DOGFIGHT
AT THE
PENTAGON

DOGFIGHT AT THE PENTAGON

Sergeant Dogs, Grumpy Cats,
Wallflower Wingmen, and Other Lunacy from
The Wall Street Journal's A-Hed Column

THE WALL STREET JOURNAL

Edited and with an introduction by
Barry Newman

HARPER

NEW YORK · LONDON · TORONTO · SYDNEY

HARPER

HarperCollins books may be purchased for educational, business, or sales promotional use. For information, please e-mail the Special Markets Department at SPsales@harpercollins.com.

Articles originally published in *The Wall Street Journal*

FIRST EDITION

Library of Congress Cataloging-in-Publication Data has been applied for.

ISBN 978-0-06-233319-3

14 15 16 17 18   OV/RRD   10 9 8 7 6 5 4 3 2 1

Contents

WORK

STUFF

Introduction

BARRY NEWMAN

What? A stock market rout? Can't the market do something surprising for a change? A revolution? Didn't we have one of those last week? Inflation. Deflation. A war surge. A storm surge. *The Wall Street Journal* lets you read all about all that. But to ease the quantitative tensions of the world's ups and downs, the *Journal* also delivers something you can't predict. It's the A-Hed.

The A-Hed, named for a headline that looked like a letter *A*, first settled into the middle column of Page One in 1941, an invention of the modern paper's first managing editor, Barney Kilgore. Mr. Kilgore and the editors who followed him thought serious business types could benefit from a little lunacy, and they knew that even in the leanest of times lunacy is never in short supply.

A while ago, the A-Hed moved to the bottom of the

front page, then it earned a home of its own on a *Journal* Web page. But no matter where it lives, the A-Hed remains one of the liveliest features around. Now a stack of them have been bundled into this book.

Those of romantic bent will find here an account of the Japanese "infidelity phone" (it keeps trysts secret) and the story of "wingmen" and "wingwomen" who escort wallflowers to nightspots and maneuver them into the arms of prospective catches. Those whose affections lean more toward dogs, cats and fish will learn how a Marine Corps bulldog got promoted to sergeant, how a bored cat acquired a Hollywood agent, and will be left wondering if a 63-pound carp named Benson died naturally in England or was the victim of foul play.

The fashion conscious have their pick of the rise of pantyhose for men (mantyhose) or an unashamed campaign to recruit youthful nudists. And then there's the story about a hairdresser, Janet Stephens, at Studio 921 Salon & Day Spa, in Baltimore. Ms. Stephens shook the foundations of ancient scholarship by proving that Roman empresses didn't wear wigs. She's a "hairdo archaeologist."

How do *Journal* reporters, supposedly consumed by issues of import, come across all this weirdness? By keeping their eyes open. Adam Entous covers the Pentagon. Walking its halls in quest of brass to buttonhole during an Afghanistan drawdown and a Syrian flare-up, his eyes fell on a portrait of a Navy man "lost at sea" in 1908. In another coup for barber-based investigative reporting, he noticed that the guy's hair looked blow-dried. Back at the office, he dropped everything (well, not quite everything) and worked for weeks to lay bare "the greatest—or perhaps only—prank in Pentagon art history."

Some articles in this collection look into things that go viral on the Internet, like an ineffably guileless review of the new Olive Garden restaurant in Grand Forks, North Dakota. The article's author, James R. Hagerty, usually writes about manufacturing out of Pittsburgh; the reviewer in Grand Forks was Marilyn Hagerty, his mother. Some other stories here went viral themselves—notably one by Russell Adams about a bunch of high school buddies from Spokane, Washington, who kept a game of tag going for 23 years.

These improbabilities are only the latest to wind up in what's become a long line of A-Hed books. "The Jilted Aardvark" came out in 1970. It had a story about five escaped wallabies, and one about hippies smoking catnip. This book is different, for one thing, because it isn't on paper. And in those old books, the stories were picked by some snickering editors. Of these stories, more than half rang up top scores on the hit lists of the *Journal*'s website. So it was snickering readers, not just the editors, who singled them out.

One final difference: *The Wall Street Journal* itself. Back when it was a stolid business paper, the A-Hed was known as "the icing on the cake." Now the *Journal*'s sections are thick with icing: Arena, Mansion, Review, Off-Duty and WSJ Magazine. It means the A-Hed has to be sweeter than ever. So curl up with your tablet and read a few. The riots and revolutions can wait.

PLAY

The Endless Game of Tag

RUSSELL ADAMS

Earlier this month, Brian Dennehy started a new job as chief marketing officer of Nordstrom Inc. In his first week, he pulled aside a colleague to ask a question: How hard is it for a nonemployee to enter the building?

Mr. Dennehy doesn't have a particular interest in corporate security. He just doesn't want to be "It."

Mr. Dennehy and nine of his friends have spent the past 23 years locked in a game of "Tag."

It started in high school when they spent their morning break darting around the campus of Gonzaga Preparatory School in Spokane, Wash. Then they moved on—to college, careers, families and new cities. But because of a reunion, a contract and someone's unusual idea to stay in touch, tag keeps pulling them closer. Much closer.

The game they play is fundamentally the same as the

schoolyard version: One player is "It" until he tags someone else. But men in their 40s can't easily chase each other around the playground, at least not without making people nervous, so this tag has a twist. There are no geographic restrictions and the game is live for the entire month of February. The last guy tagged stays "It" for the year.

That means players get tagged at work and in bed. They form alliances and fly around the country. Wives are enlisted as spies and assistants are ordered to bar players from the office.

"You're like a deer or elk in hunting season," says Joe Tombari, a high-school teacher in Spokane, who sometimes locks the door of his classroom during off-periods and checks under his car before he gets near it.

One February day in the mid-1990s, Mr. Tombari and his wife, then living in California, got a knock on the door from a friend. "Hey, Joe, you've got to check this out. You wouldn't believe what I just bought," he said, as he led the two out to his car.

What they didn't know was Sean Raftis, who was "It," had flown in from Seattle and was folded in the trunk of the Honda Accord. When the trunk was opened he leapt out and tagged Mr. Tombari, whose wife was so startled she fell backward off the curb and tore a ligament in her knee.

"I still feel bad about it," says Father Raftis, who is now a priest in Montana. "But I got Joe."

It could have been worse for Mr. Tombari. He was "It" in 1982, heading into the last day of high school. He plotted to tag a friend, who had gone home early that day. But when he got there, the friend, tipped off by another player, was sitting in his parents' car with the doors locked. There wasn't enough time to tag someone else.

"The whole thing was quite devastating," says Mr. Tombari. "I was 'It' for life."

About eight years later, some of the group were gathered for a weekend when the topic turned to Mr. Tombari and the feeble finish to his tag career. Someone came up with an idea to revive the game for one month out of the year.

Patrick Schultheis, then a first-year lawyer, drafted a "Tag Participation Agreement," which outlined the spirit of the game and the rules (no "tag-backs," or tagging the player who just tagged you). Everyone signed. The game was on.

One year early on when Mike Konesky was "It," he got confirmation, after midnight, that people were home at the house where two other players lived. He pulled up to their place at around 2 a.m., sneaked into the garage and groped around in the dark for the house door. "It was open," he says. "I'm like, 'Oh, man, I could get arrested.'"

Mr. Konesky tiptoed toward Mr. Dennehy's bedroom, burst through the door and flipped on the light. A bleary-eyed Mr. Dennehy looked up as his now-wife yelled "Run, Brian!" Mr. Konesky recalls. "There was nowhere for Brian to run."

Over the years, some of the players fanned out around the country—which curbed the action but raised the stakes. At one point, Chris Ammann was living in Boston. So Mr. Konesky dipped into his frequent-flier miles and crossed the country on the last weekend of the month. He spent the next two days in the bushes outside Mr. Ammann's apartment, sitting in his friend's favorite bar or driving up and down his street. Mr. Ammann never showed. Mr. Konesky was "It" for the year.

"I felt bad," says Mr. Ammann, who went out of town for the weekend. "I think I would have sacrificed getting tagged to spend some time with him."

The participants say Tag has helped preserve friendships that otherwise may have fizzled. Usually, though, the prospect of 11 months of ridicule overrides brotherhood.

Mr. Schultheis once refused to help a colleague change his tire, fearing the guy had been recruited to help get him tagged. He sometimes goes to Hawaii in February, partly to lessen the chances of getting tagged.

Every February, Mr. Schultheis's office manager provides security detail as well as administrative functions.

Mr. Tombari once tried to talk his way past her. "She knew it was tag time," he says. "I wasn't allowed in. Nobody got in to see him."

Mr. Konesky, a tech-company manager, is now "It" again and has had 11 months to stew. With February approaching, he has been batting around a few plans of attack. He says he likes to go after people who haven't been "It" for a while. That includes Father Raftis, who has been harder to reach since he moved to Montana but who, as several players pointed out, is a sitting duck on Sundays.

"Once I step foot outside the rectory, all bets are off," the priest says. "I have to be a little more careful."

Update

Tag, He's "It" for Another Year

RUSSELL ADAMS

It is going to be another long year for Mike Konesky.

He was tagged Thursday night while entering a school play in Spokane, Wash., with his wife and daughters, leaving too little time to get someone else before the game ended at midnight. That means next February will start the same way this one did: with Mr. Konesky as "It."

"I was completely blindsided," he said about his misfortune Thursday.

Mr. Konesky is one of 10 participants in the 24-year, no-holds-barred game of Tag chronicled in a front-page *Wall Street Journal* article in January.

The game, which is live only in February, often doesn't get going until the end of the month. This year was different, as local and national media descended upon the participants, upping the stakes. "It" changed hands at least 30 times over 28 days.

One morning in early February, Joe Caferro arrived at a television station in Seattle where some of the guys were meeting to tape an interview. While waiting in the lobby, the aerospace engineer got a text message from Patrick Schultheis to come out to his car and join him on a call with the group's agent, who has been fielding offers for the movie rights.

When his friend got near, the trunk opened and out came Joe Tombari, who tagged Mr. Caferro on the back as he yelled, "You're It, you b----!"

A few days later, Mr. Schultheis's father died unexpectedly, raising questions about how the game would proceed. Mr. Schultheis promptly announced that the funeral of Judge John Schultheis would be in play. "My dad thought this whole thing was hilarious," he said, noting Tag was a topic of their last conversation.

During the service, as Mr. Caferro walked toward the altar to take communion, he paused at the front row and grabbed his friend's shoulder. Mr. Schultheis looked up to acknowledge what he thought was a sympathetic gesture. Mr. Caferro mouthed, "You're It," and went on his way.

"It" later got back to Mr. Tombari, who enlisted his daughter in a plot to shed the label. He called Mr. Caferro's mother, who gave up the Spokane restaurant where her son would be having lunch. "There is no honor in this game," Mr. Caferro said of his mom's betrayal.

The father-daughter team dressed as an old couple and shuffled into the restaurant, where they went unnoticed until a stooped Mr. Tombari stopped at his friend's table and put his hand on his shoulder. "It took me about a second-and-a-half to recognize him," said Mr. Caferro.

As the month wound down and tensions ran high, the players raised their games. On Wednesday, Rick Bruya found out which flight Mr. Schultheis was taking home from Arizona and headed to the Seattle airport, where Mr. Bruya found a town-car driver holding a sign with his friend's name on it. But Mr. Schultheis, anticipating an ambush, had hired the car as a decoy. So while Mr. Bruya waited, Mr. Schultheis escaped through another concourse, hopped into his car and drove home.

"It cost me a hundred bucks," Mr. Schultheis said. "But it was worth it."

The tag sealing Mr. Konesky's fate happened where the tag game began: at Gonzaga Preparatory School, where the participants attended high school in the 1980s.

Mr. Bruya had managed to tag Mr. Tombari, a Gonzaga teacher, Thursday on the softball field, where Mr. Tombari coaches the high-school girls' team.

That night, Mr. Konesky had just bought the tickets and was following his family into a darkened auditorium to see a production of "The Little Mermaid," when Mr. Tombari emerged from behind the door. Mr. Konesky's wife had told Mr. Tombari where they'd be.

"I really didn't sleep [Thursday] night," Mr. Konesky said. "I can't believe I'm 'It' for another year."

Wanted: The Young and the Naked

DOUGLAS BELKIN

LOXAHATCHEE GROVES, Fla.—On a recent Friday morning, Jessi Bartoletti arrived at the Sunsport Gardens Nudist Resort here in a T-shirt and shorts.

By evening, the 19-year-old had stripped down to a string of purple Mardi Gras beads and was dancing around a bonfire with about 200 young nudists, many of them first-timers.

"I don't think I've ever felt this free," Ms. Bartoletti yelled over pounding drums.

That's good news to the nudist resort industry, which is desperate for young nudists like Ms. Bartoletti to augment its clientele of graying baby boomers.

Membership in the two big nudist umbrella groups has been flat or declining for years, prompting a youth-recruitment effort that includes reverse-strip-poker nights, volleyball tournaments, naked 5K road races and music festivals like Nudepalooza and Nudestock.

One new group, Young Nudists and Naturists of America, this month is having a naked dinner party in a loft in New York's financial district to recruit members.

"The whole lifestyle will just disappear unless we attract a younger crowd," said Nicky Hoffman, head of the Naturist Society, one of the two big organizations of U.S. nudists. "The problem is, most of these resorts aren't geared to young people. They've become like retirement homes; they've sort of calcified."

John Whitehead, 22, visited the Sunsport Gardens resort for the first time last year. He enjoyed being naked until he spotted a man his father's age he knew from work, then spent the day avoiding him.

"It's not that I have anything against old people," Mr. Whitehead said. "I just don't really want to hang out with them at the pool."

In 1929, six men and women in their twenties attended what is believed to have been the first nudist retreat, organized in upstate New York by German immigrant Kurt Barthel.

In Mr. Barthel's homeland, nudism had taken root among young people as an expression of physical fitness and harmony with nature. In the U.S., it found controversy.

Nudists meeting in private in New York were arrested and charged with indecent exposure. In 1935, a crowd beat up a dozen nudists in northern New Jersey.

In the 1960s, public nudity gained wider acceptance. Morley Schloss, now the 69-year-old majority shareholder of Sunsport Gardens, skinny-dipped for the first time at the Woodstock Music Festival in 1969.

"I stood there in front of Mother Nature and all those people and said, 'This is me! This is who I am!'" Mr. Schloss recalls. "It changed my life."

Nudist resorts sprang up across the country. There are more than 250 today, plus cruises and other events making up a $440 million business, says the American Association for Nude Recreation.

But AANR and Naturist Society membership stopped growing years ago, mainly because many people now in their twenties and thirties don't appear interested in joining.

Young people have largely turned their backs on nudist camps, favoring instead public nudist spots like Hippie Hollow in Austin, Texas; Baker Beach in San Francisco or Haulover Beach in Miami, a "clothing optional" stretch of sand at the city's northern edge.

One reason: Private nudist clubs tend to be geared toward retirees.

Pools close at sundown. Body piercings are prohibited. Some older nudists complain that younger ones keep them up with late-night cavorting. Mostly, though, youngsters appear not to be eager to socialize regularly with folks the age of their grandparents.

So the AANR and the Naturist Society have asked their younger members to reach out to their peers and think of ways to make them feel that undressing in front of strangers is wonderful. Florida Young Naturists, Vita Nuda and other young nudist groups have since formed.

Vita Nuda organizes most of the young people who attend Nudepalooza each fall at the Cypress Cove Nudist Resort and Spa in Kissimmee, Fla., said resort owner Ted Hadley.

"We've been looking for years to reach out to that demographic and it's been a lot of brick walls," Mr. Hadley said. "It took a group of young nudists to do it on their own."

Robbe White, 27 years old, attended a winter festival at Sunsport Gardens in 2009 and was one of a handful of people younger than 35.

"I thought, 'This is ridiculous,'" he said. "I wanted to bring people my own age in to see what it was about."

He founded the Florida Young Naturists, opened a Facebook account and organized the first Spring Break Bash at Sunsport Gardens for people under 30.

The inaugural Bash attracted 75 people. This year, 140 young nudists showed up for a free weekend on the grass-and-sand grounds of Sunsport Gardens, including a "midnight skinny dip and blacklight party."

One Friday morning, guests pulled off the dirt road that separates the Everglades from the rustic, 40-acre resort. A middle-aged man wearing only a ponytail and glasses sat behind a desk registering people. Signs informed visitors that there were seven types of poisonous snakes in the area and that photography was forbidden.

Guests under 30 were handed colored wristbands to give them access to an area separate from the rest of the resort. The idea was to keep them from feeling uncomfortable around older guests.

"No one wants to feel like eye candy," said Kathleen Kraft, a 27-year-old organizer handing out the wristbands.

Some young guests disrobed immediately. Others hesitated or covered themselves with towels.

Ms. Bartoletti said she felt a surge of anxiety as she prepared to disrobe in public for the first time.

At the pool, she saw a sign saying nudity is mandatory in the water. "Well, this is what I came here for," she thought. Off came the towel.

Pup tents went up. Several bands in various stages of undress began to play. Vendors sold tapestries, fruit smoothies and jewelry.

On Saturday, some of the much older residents and visitors joined the younger guests for volleyball, a mainstay of traditional nudist colonies.

"The barriers between people just fall away when you're nude," Ms. Kraft said. "It's like watching chains falling off."

Ms. Bartoletti, who is starting college in May, said she felt as if she'd known her fellow nudists for weeks. Her only complaint was the mosquitoes.

"I woke up this morning and put on a shirt to keep them off me," she said.

Walk the Prank

ADAM ENTOUS

WASHINGTON—In a Pentagon hallway hung an austere portrait of a Navy man lost at sea in 1908, with his brass buttons, blue-knit uniform and what looks like meticulously blow-dried hair.

Wait. Blow-dried hair?

The portrait of "Ensign Chuck Hord," framed in the heavy gilt typical of government offices, may be the greatest—or perhaps only—prank in Pentagon art history. "Chuck Hord" can't be found in Navy records of the day. It isn't even a real painting. The textured, 30-year-old photo is actually of Capt. Eldridge Hord III, 53 years old, known to friends as "Tuck," a military retiree with a beer belly and graying hair who lives in Burke, Va.

Most military officers who climb the ranks or command

daring battles only dream of having a portrait hang in a corridor of power at the Pentagon alongside the likes of Patton, Nimitz and Eisenhower. Capt. Hord's made its way to the Pentagon's C-ring hallway via several parties, an alliance of British and Canadian military officers and a clandestine, predawn operation later dubbed "THE PROJECT."

The picture came into existence after Capt. Hord graduated from the U.S. Naval Academy in 1982. During a visit to then-Ensign Hord's hometown of Kingsport, Tenn., his proud parents suggested he sit for a formal portrait. Wearing midshipman's garb and an Annapolis class ring, he posed for the town's best-known photographer in front of a cloth screen with his arms resting on an antique-looking chair.

The photographer liked the photo so much he framed several copies and hung them in stores around Kingsport to advertise his business, Capt. Hord says. Some were textured and signed to resemble oil paintings.

Colleagues say Capt. Hord has always been something of a prankster. His 1982 Naval Academy yearbook says he "never let academic problems interfere with his two favorite pastimes, drinking beer in dives and playing the ponies."

After his graduation, he went to sea, captained a guided-missile frigate in the Pacific hunting for drug runners and studied at the National War College.

In his first stint at the Pentagon starting in 1997, his slapstick sense of humor earned him the title of the "George Costanza" of the Joint Staff, a reference to a character from the sitcom "Seinfeld."

Over the next 20 years, some of the portraits found their way back to the Hord family. In 2004, Capt. Hord says his sister surprised him by bringing the largest one—3 feet tall—to a party at his Virginia house. She left it by the front door.

Capt. Hord at the time was director of the Multinational Interagency division, a new Pentagon office designed to coordinate military logistics between the U.S. and its closest allies.

Office colleagues say Capt. Hord developed close bonds with his British, Canadian and Australian counterparts. Their office boasted its own beer fridge.

Several of Capt. Hord's work colleagues attended the 2004 party, including a British captain who smuggled the portrait into his car and put it on display at the office. Capt. Hord, amused, called it an act of "buffoonery."

The portrait then started making surprise appearances at events when Capt. Hord was in attendance. It attended his 2005 farewell party when he left the Pentagon office to take a new post in Diego Garcia, an Indian Ocean atoll where the Navy has a base.

He left the portrait with his officemates, who placed it on the wall above his old desk.

In 2009, British Naval Capt. Mike Bullock, now a commodore, lugged the heavy portrait past armed Pentagon security guards, onto a subway train and to Capt. Hord's retirement party at Washington's Navy Memorial.

"I was expecting to be questioned by the Pentagon police why I was taking the picture out of the building and instead was helped through the barrier!" Commodore Bullock recalled.

After the party, Capt. Hord refused to take ownership of the portrait, Commodore Bullock said. "I think the contrast between the Ensign Hord and the retiring Capt. Hord was too much for him!" he added.

Back on the wall in the office, visitors often asked who it depicted. "They all looked at it and said, 'Man, what year was that? It looks like the 1800s,'" said Canadian Lt. Col. Brook Bangsboll.

That was the lightbulb moment. On one of his last days at the Pentagon, Lt. Col. Bangsboll went to a jewelry shop to have a brass plaque engraved, egged on by colleagues and co-conspirators. "We didn't know what to do so we said, 'Let's just lose him at sea,'" Lt. Col. Bangsboll said. "It makes it interesting and kind of mysterious."

He kept the circumstances of the ensign's death vague because he thought some nosy Navy historian would spot the ruse if the plaque cited a specific battle.

The jeweler made a typo, engraving "Chuck" instead of "Tuck." Lt. Col. Bangsboll felt that was fitting, given the surreptitious nature of his endeavor. It read:

ENS CHUCK HORD

USNA, CIRCA 1898

LOST AT SEA 1908

Lt. Col. Bangsboll scouted the halls for the right spot. He planned to put the portrait in a foyer dedicated to logistics—the office's specialty—but feared those responsible for displays in the area would catch on.

He settled on a previously unadorned hallway which gets less foot traffic. At 6:15 a.m. on July 29, 2011, Lt. Col. Bangsboll spirited the portrait to the hallway and drove a large screw into the wall.

"The place was quiet," he recalls. "No one noticed."

For the next seven months, the portrait attracted little attention. One Pentagon official, as he walked by the photo, said it had never crossed his mind to look twice.

Unfortunately for Capt. Hord, the gag is up.

After *The Wall Street Journal* asked Pentagon officials about the long-lost sailor's suspiciously modern hairstyle, Lt. Col. Bangsboll, who has returned to Ottawa, received what he described as a "fairly frantic email" from an American major still in the liaison office.

"They're onto you, sir," U.S. Army Maj. Brooke Stull told Lt. Col. Bangsboll. "We've had to take the picture down."

A Pentagon official explained by email why Capt. Hord's picture was removed from the public hallway. "There's an approval process for Pentagon portraits and this beautiful picture has not been approved for display :)"

Capt. Hord makes no apologies.

"A little bit of alcohol and a whole big dose of irreverence plays into it," he said. "Plus you feel like you're getting one over on somebody."

But he also seems a bit sad. "I started that office and this was going to put me in perpetuity in the Pentagon," he said with a sigh.

The portrait, whose frame was badly damaged after its removal from the wall, now sits on the floor of the office where Capt. Hord once worked, leaning against a cubicle wall.

JULIAN E. BARNES CONTRIBUTED TO THIS ARTICLE.

The World's Biggest Liars

ALISTAIR MACDONALD

Glen Boylan

SANTON BRIDGE, England—In this tiny village last week, Glen Boylan came to spin stories in a local pub, as the English are wont to do. On a rain-lashed night, Mr. Boylan's tale involved being offered a mayonnaise and peanut butter sandwich by a good Samaritan—Prince Charles—who happened to be passing through.

This was no ordinary night of pub banter, however. At the Bridge Inn, Mr. Boylan was competing in the World's Biggest Liar competition, the village's annual celebration of dishonesty. Competitors' tall tales are judged on imagination, presentation and sheer chutzpah.

But in recent years, the contest's popularity has attracted more competitors from outside the area to Cumbria, in northwest England, one of the country's most remote regions. That has exposed an ugly truth for Cumbrians: The best fibbers are increasingly coming from other parts of Britain, and even other parts of the world.

"Anyone from anywhere is welcome at the contest—enter and spin a yarn—they are just not welcome to win it," said Mark Samson, an unemployed construction worker who had come to cheer on the local lad, Mr. Boylan, a 46-year-old worker at a nearby nuclear-power plant.

Cumbria isn't alone in trying to protect its local rituals from the outside world. Few countries celebrate eccentricity like the British, who in various places hold contests for snail racing, bog snorkeling, toe wrestling and a World Gurning Championship, in which contestants compete to contort their faces into the most grotesque expressions.

But events that originated in once-isolated villages are attracting ever bigger crowds, and, in some cases, being commercialized, leaving locals worried about their ties to the regional traditions that engendered them. In the village of Brockworth, Gloucestershire, some have rebelled over what they see as the hijacking of an event in which competitors chase an eight-pound cheese rolled down a steep, grassy slope. The last two years' "official" contests were cancelled after organizers for the 200-year-old event complained of being threatened and abused for introducing an entry fee of about $30.

In Ashborne, increasing numbers of "tourists" join in the Royal Shrovetide Football Match, a riotous two-day cross between rugby and soccer that has few rules and uses the entire English Midlands town as its playing field. But outsiders are discouraged from scoring in a game that has pitted the town's south and north sides since the 12th century.

The liars' competition began in the 19th century as a tribute to local pub landlord Will Ritson, whose famous fibs included tales of turnips so big that local farmers carved them out to make cow sheds. Legend has it that one senior church man won the prize after standing up to say he had never told a lie; some suspect that tale is itself a lie.

The threat of globalization arrived in Stanton Bridge in 2005, when a South African, Abrie Kruger, won the contest and ushered in a string of wins for non-Cumbrians. After Mr. Kruger was announced the winner, spectators broke into a chorus of "Rule, Britannia," a song of British patriotism.

Then, in 2006, London comedian Sue Perkins won with a tale about flatulent sheep causing a hole in the ozone layer. Ms. Perkins was booed upon winning, but retorts: "If they want to call it the World's Biggest Liar, then the world has to be eligible."

This year, six Cumbrians and five interlopers squared off in a region whose picturesque, hilly landscape inspired tales of talking rabbits from Beatrix Potter and opium-induced poetry from Samuel Taylor Coleridge.

The first of the non-Cumbrian competitors was Rebecca Purves, an economist from Cheltenham, in southwest England. "Women cannot and do not lie," she said, before telling a fraudulent tale of shopping and false price tags.

Subdued applause for Ms. Purves made way for the raucous cheers that heralded John Graham, a local farmer and seven-time winner of this liars' Olympiad. After 24 contests, the self-styled "Johnny Liar" said he is "running out of lies." But he told one that had him flying with sea gulls, swimming with salmon and shooting a pig he mistook for a ghost.

For Mr. Boylan, appearing on the same stage as Mr. Graham is an honor. "You taught me to lie," Mr. Boylan told him later, saying he had learned his trade watching Mr. Graham perform.

Mr. Graham believes the competition has changed as outsiders turn it into more of a professional comedy show than the "good, honest" lying of old. "They are comedians, not liars," said Mr. Graham, the dirt from a day's farming still under his fingernails.

Two-time winner Howard Christie, a local landlord, laments the passing of an earlier era of fibbing and believes strong local dialects like Mr. Graham's put off judges who want broadcastable accents to increase the appeal of the competition beyond Cumbria.

John Jackson, a regional mayor and one of seven judges, denies there are biases. "I just pick the best lie," he said.

In last week's competition, more controversy was generated when Scotsman Michael O'Rourke was accused of plagiarizing his routine—about scientists trying to erase the "ginger gene" that "creates" redheads—from a famous British comedian's routine. "That's a lie," said Mr. O'Rourke.

Then it was Mr. Boylan's turn. His hair was spiked, his shirt, sweaty. "You are not going to believe this," Mr. Boylan said, before telling of how he lost all his money betting on a snail race, despite following Prince Charles's advice to remove the snail's shell to make it more aerodynamic. Finding him hungry and broke, Mr. Boylan said, the heir to the British throne took pity on him and shared his lunch of mayonnaise and peanut butter sandwiches.

As the judges deliberated, Mr. Boylan was besieged by jubilant supporters. "It's coming home, it's coming home," Mr. Samson chanted, aping an England soccer song that bemoans the country's lack of recent success at the sport it created.

When the judges returned, the jovial crowd fell silent, a region's hopes hinging on the sheet of paper held in the emcee's hand. The news was good: Mr. Boylan was crowned the winner, and fellow Cumbrians took silver and bronze. "A clean sweep for Cumbria," somebody shouted.

Gazing afterward at the large, silver trophy, Mr. Boylan felt emotional. "It's back in Cumbria, where it belongs," he said. "That is where the world's biggest liars come from."

That's not what they thought at Mr. O'Rourke's table. Mr. O'Rourke "didn't win it just because he is a Scotsman," said Colin O'Brien, a construction worker from Glasgow. "Anyone who says differently is lying."

Hey, Bro, That's My Little Pony!

VAUHINI VARA AND ANN ZIMMERMAN

BERKELEY, Calif.—Fifteen young men in this hotbed of activism gathered at an Indian restaurant on a recent Sunday and made an appeal: Could the waiter please switch the TV from the news to "My Little Pony"?

Then the men heaped their plates with curry and clustered around tables to absorb the Pony cartoon, share trivia about the characters and play show-and-tell with the various plastic Pony toys they had brought along.

Meet the self-described "bronies."

The object of the bronies' fascination is "My Little Pony: Friendship is Magic," a remake of a 1980s animated

TV show for preadolescent girls featuring plucky, candy-colored equines.

After the show launched in October 2010, video clips began appearing on 4chan, a website that largely draws geeky, tech-savvy guys. Before long, the bronies were born. They started holding local get-togethers, from Seattle to Brooklyn, where they recognized each other by the paper Pony cut-outs tucked in their shirt pockets. They'd discuss the latest shenanigans of Ponies with names like Twilight Sparkle and Fluttershy.

Some bronies say they got hooked on the high-quality animation. Others felt they identified with the four-legged stars that flaunt luxurious, pony-tail-like manes. "The characters aren't one-dimensional," said 15-year-old Christian Leisner, a brony in the Berkeley group. "They have flaws, they have backgrounds they're ashamed of."

Bronies—a mash-up of "bro" and "ponies"—established a quarterly New York convention, called BroNYCon, this year. They've spawned at least two Pony-themed websites and enjoy a thriving subculture of artists whose creations include Pony-inspired music and their own writings about Twilight Sparkle and the gang.

Jessica Blank, a 32-year-old computer programmer who is BroNYCon's organizer, says people inevitably ask her whether the bronies—three-quarters of whom are male—are gay. "Actually, the overwhelming majority are straight," she says.

Bronies say their hobby has nothing to do with their sexuality or gender. "I don't care about showing to the world that I am masculine," says Jason Subhani, a 19-year-old college student in Astoria, N.Y. A Pony poster on his bedroom wall mingles with images of heavy-metal icons.

At the recent informal Berkeley gathering, Quinn Johnson, an 18-year-old freshman at the city's University of California campus, showed a Rubik's cube he had customized with homemade "My Little Pony" stickers. Michael Boveda, a 16-year-old high-school junior, proffered a plastic Pony carefully transported in a plastic food container. "I didn't want to ruin the hair," he explained.

The group included four "Pegasisters," as the small minority of female bronies sometimes call themselves in this male-dominated world. Voices escalated, and Ohad Kanne, a 27-year-old studying videogame design, crossed to the TV and turned up the volume on "My Little Pony: Friendship is Magic."

It wasn't supposed to be this way. When Hasbro Inc. and Discovery Communications Inc. revived the "My Little Pony" franchise on a new television network called The Hub, an executive told investors the remake was for "the three- to six-year-old girl and her mom, who has fond memories of 'My Little Pony' from her childhood."

The Ponies confront knotty challenges—such as an invasion of adorable but hungry insects called Parasprites—and report to a ruler named Princess Celestia about the life lessons they learn.

This is the sort of thing discussed at Equestria Daily, a

brony website with links to such enthusiast-pleasers as free Pony coloring books. Shaun Scotellaro, its 23-year-old founder, says he cut back on his community-college classes to run the site out of his parents' house in Glendale, Ariz., and has since become a cult hero.

"Growing up, 'My Little Pony' was basically on my list, being a boy, of things I'd probably hate," says Mr. Subhani, the college student from Queens. Then he found the remake, he says, and "before I knew it, I was going on Equestria Daily more than any other news website."

Mr. Subhani tried to get his rock-band mates to play some Pony-inspired covers. They declined, so he formed a new band of bronies called Neighslayer, in which he plays guitar-heavy renditions of such "My Little Pony" songs as "Art of the Dress."

The show's producers have caught on to the phenomenon. This September, "My Little Pony" supervising director Jayson Thiessen was a special guest at BroNY-Con, which drew 300 bronies to a studio in Chinatown. Mr. Thiessen, 33, addressed a raucous crowd of men, Neighslayer performed and the guy in the best Pony costume won an award.

Later, Mr. Thiessen wrote on Twitter that the enthusiasm "completely floored me!"

In an email, a Hasbro spokeswoman said of the bronies: "From what we've seen, they are a small group of 'My Little Pony' fans who don't necessarily fit what one might expect to be the brand's target audience."

Sales of "My Little Pony" merchandise are growing, says Hasbro, which declined to provide figures or comment on who, exactly, is buying the stuff.

The Hub Chief Executive Margaret Loesch said she is aware of the show's strong following among young males, but says the majority of adult viewers are still overwhelmingly female. "I think part of why it resonates is the funky, flying mystical creatures," she says. "The combination of plenty of action and heart gives it broad appeal."

Some bronies disdain Hasbro's Pony figurines, which they find too commercial and not "show-accurate." A pet peeve: On TV, Princess Celestia is a heavenly white, but the toy is cotton-candy pink. So the bronies frequently buy unofficial merchandise from each other, including treasures such as pipe-cleaner Ponies.

Leaving the Berkeley gathering, bronies discussed loved ones' reactions. "My sisters say, 'What's wrong with you?'" said Mr. Kanne, who wore a Pony T-shirt. "Luckily, we have this community that understands."

Update

Bronies Still Riding High

VAUHINI VARA

The bronies have been going strong since the article was published in 2011.

The Bronies of Northern California—the group that met at the Berkeley, Calif., restaurant—now has 854 members, up from 143 when the *Journal* first reported on them, said co-organizer Nicolo Tech. Ohad Kanne, a rank-and-file member quoted in the article, today organizes the group. Since the early days, he says, some of the group's first members have left.

"Some of those have been busy, some rarely come to meet us anymore, we keep in touch with some of them," said the 29-year-old. "The group is constantly changing."

Shaun Scotellaro, 25, still runs the Equestria Daily fan site for bronies—still out of his parents' house, though not out of financial necessity but because "I have a pretty tight family that gives each other space."

Jayson Thiessen, supervising director for the program, has only gotten more involved in the world of bronies and ponies. He said he directed a My Little Ponies film that premiered at the Los Angeles Film Festival in June. He said he was, once again, "floored" by the response.

Others like Jason Subhani, 21, have drifted from the world of bronies. He said his brony band, Neighslayer, went through some lineup changes and performed at a couple of conventions, but gradually, the members disbanded as they "kinda lost interest in ponies." Today, he said, "I hang out with punks and anime fans."

The Hershberger Award's 40-Year Secret

RACHEL BACHMAN

In the winter of 1972, Steven Noll and three sports-junkie friends at the College of William & Mary in Williamsburg, Va., were nursing two gripes.

One was the proliferation of All-America teams in college basketball—the annual awards given to standout players by sports magazines and journalist groups.

The other was the belief they shared that none of those teams would ever recognize the star player in their midst—William & Mary's own Mike Arizin, 6-foot-5 shooting guard and small forward.

So the college buddies hatched a plan. They made up a fictitious professional organization and called it the National Association of Collegiate Basketball Writers. They then created an All-America team of their very own, naming the top 15 rookie players in the nation.

In March 1973, they mailed official-looking certificates to the universities where the winners played. Finally, the four men, long-haired juniors who had never published a word about college basketball, told the Associated Press about the award. The next day, stories about it appeared in newspapers all over the country.

For 40 years, the men told almost nobody about the fake award, which they gave out just once. Now, as this year's NCAA Final Four starts Saturday, the men are telling their story with heads held high.

"Are we proud of this? Oh yeah," said Mr. Noll, now a senior lecturer in the history department at the University of Florida. "I think it's fun stuff."

The pranksters went to great lengths to make the award believable. They spent hours at the library, paging through newspaper box scores to help them select recipients. They designed stationery with a slogan: "Serving the Sport." They sent correspondence from Mr. Noll's parents' address in Garden City, N.Y., for big-city authority.

"My mother thought we'd go to prison for mail fraud," Mr. Noll said.

Paul Pavlich, a co-conspirator, said that plotting the scam was as painstaking as an ascent of Mount Everest.

Their preparation paid off. Newspapers printed their fabricated details. An article in the *Miami Herald* announced the all-rookie team as "selected by the nation's college basketball writers." The *Hartford Courant* noted that North Carolina State's David Thompson was "the only unanimous choice." News of the award also appeared in the *Los Angeles Times*, *Atlanta Constitution*, *New York Daily News* and elsewhere.

"It would be impossible to reconstruct 40 years ago, but I find it hard to imagine this could ever happen again at the AP," says Paul Colford, the AP's chief spokesman.

The hoax lasted longer than Notre Dame linebacker Manti Te'o's girlfriend. Until this week, some of the All-America rookie award winners still had no idea that it was all a joke.

Louis "Sweet Lou" Dunbar was a rookie award first-team member at the University of Houston before his 24-year playing career with the Harlem Globetrotters, where he's now a coach. Mr. Dunbar laughed when a reporter told him of the prank. He compared it to famous Globetrotter tricks: "This is right up there with the water and the confetti," he said.

The hoaxers named the award for the late Leo G. Hershberger—a crusty, cigar-chomping New York sportswriter. He was a figment, too.

The name made the award stand out to James "Fly" Williams, a Hershberger winner for Austin Peay State University in Clarksville, Tenn. Mr. Williams, reached by telephone, laughed when he learned of the hoax: "Amazing . . . something else."

Several players who won the award went on to greatness: Indiana University's Quinn Buckner was co-captain of the team that won the 1976 national championship. John Lucas had a 14-year pro career and coached in the NBA. North Carolina State's Mr. Thompson is in the Basketball Hall of Fame.

At the time Roger Valdiserri, the sports-information director at the University of Notre Dame, sent the "association" a thank-you letter. A few years after that, Mr. Noll and a co-conspirator, Reed Bohne, were driving through Indiana and stopped at Notre Dame. Mr. Noll posed as an ardent fan from England, asking to see the school's All-America awards.

Mr. Valdiserri welcomed the men into his office, where the Hershberger Award was hanging in a frame on the wall, and the men gleefully snapped pictures.

Mr. Valdiserri's secretary then was the wife of a Notre Dame quarterback and invited the men to join her and her husband for a drink. That was how Mr. Noll and Mr. Bohne say they came to meet future Notre Dame and Super Bowl legend Joe Montana, Mr. Noll prattling on in a British accent to keep up the ruse.

This week, Mr. Valdiserri said he remembered meeting the men and guffawed about what they had done. Kim Moses, now divorced from Mr. Montana, didn't recall the men specifically but said Notre Dame was a very social place and that she "very likely" introduced them to her famous former husband.

During the 2007–2008 academic year, Mr. Noll had a freshman basketball player in his American history class named Jai Lucas—the son of John Lucas, a Hershberger Award winner. "I debated whether to say something," Mr. Noll recalled. "I never did." Jai Lucas said Mr. Noll is still one of his favorite professors.

Only once, the hoaxers say, did they spill the beans to a player. In the late 1970s, Mr. Bohne waited tables at a restaurant frequented by Detroit Pistons players, and one day happened to serve former University of Alabama center Leon Douglas, a Hershberger winner. Mr. Bohne says he told Mr. Douglas the story and the player "was dumbfounded." Reached this week, Mr. Douglas, men's basketball coach at Tuskegee University in Alabama, said he remembered getting the award but didn't recall meeting Mr. Bohne.

Today, two of the pranksters are academics. Two of the men have worked for the government. Mr. Bohne is a regional director for the National Oceanic and Atmospheric Administration living in Savannah, Ga., and Tom Duncan, who lives in Fairfax, Va., is retired after 30 years as a lawyer.

Mr. Arizin, the former William & Mary player, mused that his "greatest college sports award turned out to be a fraud," but said that's OK by him. "I'm sort of flattered," he said.

William & Mary's current president, Taylor Reveley, said the school has been fostering creativity for more than 300 years and that "these four students obviously fall in that grand tradition."

Fishy Story

ALISTAIR MACDONALD AND PAUL SONNE

TANSOR, England—In the land of Sherlock Holmes and Agatha Christie, it has fallen to a taxidermist to uncover whether foul play is to blame for the corpse found floating in a lake here late last month: Benson, the legendary 52-pound carp whose untimely death has captivated a nation's anglers.

For years, Benson was a catch-and-release attraction in Bluebell Lakes, a private fishing complex. Benson was a normal-size carp when she was placed in Kingfisher Lake 16 years ago. The lakes' owner, Tony Bridgefoot, noticed Benson's propensity to pack on the pounds and groomed her for stardom. For years, Mr. Bridgefoot was able to claim that Benson was the U.K.'s largest common carp, her appeal bolstered by bright-orange scales that seemed painted on and perfect lips.

The result was a plus-size phenomenon. Fishermen from as far afield as Germany trekked to this lake hoping to hook a fish the size of a family dog. Benson was caught and put back in the lake 63 times, hitting a high weight of 64 pounds two years ago.

But at 2 p.m. on July 28, Mr. Bridgefoot, at his holiday home in Norfolk, took a disturbing call from his grandson, Jimmy: a large fish body had been found floating in one of his lakes.

"You'd better get back here, it looks like it's Benson," Mr. Bridgefoot remembers being told. Mr. Bridgefoot got in his car and drove home. Sure enough, Benson was sleeping with the fishes, so to speak.

"My heart just dropped," Mr. Bridgefoot recalls.

Benson attracted attention across Britain for the sheer spectacle of her girth. Among fishermen, it was a more emotional issue.

"Within the fishing fraternity, she was like a film star, like Raquel Welch," said Dave Wilmot, a fisherman from Nottingham, standing on the shores of Kingfisher Lake in a pouring rain this week. "Like Sophia Loren," another angler piped in, and "equally difficult to catch."

But Benson's demise also set off an investigation to determine the cause of the 25-year-old's death.

Carp, it turns out, can live to 60, and when Mr. Bridgefoot found the traces of raw tiger nuts on the banks of Kingfisher Lake, and an empty bag nearby, he began to wonder whether his legendary fish had been poisoned by one of her pursuers. These nuts, a banned substance at Bluebell Lakes, are used to tempt fish to the surface, but they can prove toxic to a carp if they have been kept in moist conditions and not cooked.

"I had quite a rapport with the fish, and when she was caught, I used to talk to her, tell her to go make one more angler happy and look after herself in the meantime," Mr. Bridgefoot recalled on Thursday. Benson was also big business, and Bluebell Lakes was already suffering in the recession. Mr. Bridgefoot estimates around 40% of Bluebell Lakes' anglers came to try to catch the leviathan fish.

Word of Benson's demise spread quickly among her pursuers. At 6 p.m. Tuesday, James Piggott received a text message from a friend: "I've got some bad news for you—Benson is dead." It took three more calls from friends to convince Mr. Piggott it was true. For eight years, he fished alternate weekends—plus weeks of vacations—in an unsuccessful bid to catch Benson. Just weeks ago, Mr. Piggott was tantalizingly close, friends say, but Benson broke free and now she will never be his.

If it was poison, Mr. Piggott—and a lot of other people—want to know who did it.

"They should be banned from fishing," he said.

But who plays coroner to a carp? That afternoon, Barry Williams, a taxidermist with some zoology training, was mounting a red stag head when he took a call from Mr. Bridgefoot.

Mr. Bridgefoot first encountered Mr. Williams years

ago and the two bonded when Mr. Bridgefoot took a stuffed alligator off the taxidermist's hands after a client had refused to pay for it.

Now, Mr. Bridgefoot had two jobs for Mr. Williams: Find out what killed the fish he described as like "a hand-crafted sculpture"—and stuff Benson so she could be mounted on the wall of Mr. Bridgefoot's fishing lodge.

Benson's corpse currently sits in a freezer at Mr. Bridgefoot's house, where it will stay till Mr. Williams drives down on Friday to pick it up. By Sunday morning, with Benson thawed, photographed and measured, Mr. Williams expects to get to work.

Peter Burgess, an expert in fish health at the University of Plymouth, England, wonders whether a taxidermist can solve the case, likening it to sending a dead relative to a butcher to determine the cause of death. He says that clues are vanishing by the hour, because freezing the fish damages the tissue.

Dr. Burgess, a veteran of "countless" fish autopsies, has all but ruled out some typical fish-death suspects such as low oxygen levels in the lake or infections; no other corpses were found with Benson.

The lack of other carcasses has also led Dr. Burgess, and others, to question the toxic-nut theory. This, too, would have likely claimed other victims.

Mr. Bridgefoot disagrees. Benson "was a very greedy girl" and may have eaten the entire feed, he says.

On examining a photo of Benson, Dr. Burgess thinks

he may have one clue: her large gut. A healthy carp should be a lot more streamlined, but carp in fishing lakes often suffer from poor fatty diets due to baits, like cooked tiger nuts, that anglers use to tempt them.

The culprit then may not be one angler, but all of them. Likewise, the stress Benson suffered from anglers plucking her out of the water 63 times may have finally caught up with her, a potential cause even Mr. Bridgefoot acknowledges.

Benson's diet is a factor that Mr. Williams, who first started taxidermy at age 14 by mounting a rat, has already earmarked to examine. Fatty deposits on the liver would point to that, he says. Other signs he will look for include a "badly discolored digestive tract," which would suggest poisoning.

Mr. Williams doesn't want to preempt his investigation but says he believes the likely cause was complications due to pregnancy. Over the years, he has had more than 10 carp on his table, and in most cases the cause of death was eggs blocking up the uterus and causing infections.

"By Sunday afternoon I'll have a good idea of what went wrong" for Benson, says Mr. Williams.

On the banks of Kingfisher Lake, fishermen reminisced by the spot where Benson's lifeless body was reeled in for the final time.

Ray Armstrong, a fisherman from Birmingham, spent seven years trying to catch Benson and finally succeeded at 2 a.m. a year and a half ago. "It was like winning the lottery . . . a magical night," he said.

Update

Benson's Killer Identified

ALISTAIR MACDONALD

Benson the giant carp was probably not a victim of foul play, the taxidermist charged with examining her sudden death said. Instead, the fish likely died from reproductive complications. Barry Williams, a taxidermist from England's midlands who was asked to explore Benson's death, said that, while preparing her to be mounted, he found evidence that the fish had been spawning. Eggs can block up a fish's oviduct, leading to infections that can kill.

When Online Reviews
Are a Joke

MICHAEL M. PHILLIPS

"A Million Random Digits"

What is it about the book "A Million Random Digits with 100,000 Normal Deviates" that brings out the wiseguy in people?

Rand Corp.'s 600-page paperback, which delivers exactly what it promises, sells for $64.60 on Amazon.com. Yet 400 people have submitted online Amazon reviews, most of them mocking the 60-year-old reference book for mathematicians, pollsters and lottery administrators.

"Almost perfect," said one reviewer. "But with so many terrific random digits, it's a shame they didn't sort them, to make it easier to find the one you're looking for."

Five stars from this commenter: "[T]he first thing I thought to myself after reading chapter one was, 'Look out, Harry Potter!'"

Several reviewers complained that while most of the numbers in the book appeared satisfactorily random, the pages themselves were in numerical order.

Amazon's online superstore has become the unlikely stage for 21st-century amateur comedy, where thousands of customers have submitted reviews for products ranging from the self-explanatory explanatory book "How to

Avoid Huge Ships" to the Hutzler 571 banana slicer, a yellow plastic banana-shaped device that cuts bananas into even slices.

Rand said its long list of random numbers, first published in 1955, is one of its all-time best sellers. "It's a tool of some sort, but it's beyond my clear understanding," a Rand spokesman admitted.

One Amazon reviewer panned a real-life copycat publication called "A Million Random Digits THE SEQUEL: with Perfectly Uniform Distribution." "Let's be honest, 4735942 is just a rehashed version of 64004382, and 32563233 is really nothing more than 97132654 with an accent."

"We are always amazed by the creativity of our customers," said an Amazon spokeswoman.

The late John W. Trimmer's earnest guide to maritime safety, "How to Avoid Huge Ships," won a prize for oddest title of 1992 and is now out of print. Online, though, it's the gift gag that keeps on giving.

"Reads like a whodunit," said one five-star reviewer, joking, "I bought 'How to Avoid Huge Ships' as a companion to Capt. Trimmer's other excellent titles: 'How to Avoid a Train' and 'How to Avoid the Empire State Building.'" More than 1,500 people said that review helped them decide whether to buy the book.

"Saved My Life and My Sanity," praised a 2012 reviewer. "For about 8 months now I have noticed that a huge ship has been stalking me . . . I was fearful because my parents were killed by a big ship when they went out one day 4 years ago to walk the dog, and I have nightmares about it to this day."

That reviewer gave the book four out of five stars. "I do have to deduct a star because this book did not come out in time to save my parents."

Many "Huge Ships" shoppers also viewed "The 2009–2014 Outlook for Wood Toilet Seats in Greater China," a $495 e-book by Icon Group International, which publishes computer-generated market reports.

"I was thinking, 'Sweet! Finally a version of Outlook that will run on my wooden Chinese toilet seats!!' " wrote one disappointed reviewer. "Little did I know this has **NOTHING** to do with Outlook for Windows or any other Microsoft product."

Putative buyers of the "Fresh Whole Rabbit" ($45.90) appear taken aback by what arrives in the mail. "It's Dead!" complained a California reviewer. "I bought this for my kids since they wanted a bunny for Easter . . . They cried the whole day and it really made the Easter Egg hunt a downer . . . It may have been alive when it was first packed but the box didn't have any holes in it."

Philippe Desandre, French-born chairman of the rabbit purveyor, LeVillage.com, suspects animal-rights activists are behind the flurry of comments and photos posted to the Los Angeles company's Amazon page. "It's because in America rabbit is considered a pet, which is not the case in Europe," he said.

Nearly 11,500 people found helpful this three-star review of the Images Scientific Instruments Uranium Ore sample: "I purchased this product 4.47 billion years ago and when I opened it today, it was half empty."

John Iovine, president of the Staten Island company, has adopted an any-buzz-is-good-buzz attitude toward the endless radiation jokes. "After 100 or 200 [reviews], you just have to give in and just let it go," he said.

Besides, an Amazon manager wrote Mr. Iovine congratulating him for his uranium's "cult status."

The Hutzler 571 banana slicer—which can be pressed onto a banana to slice even pieces—has generated 4,000 reviews. "I had to return this product because it is only for bananas that curve to the right and I can only find bananas that curve to the left," a one-star reviewer complained.

"Imagine my disappointment when I opened the box to discover that they hadn't sent the power cord," wrote another. "This may be the best thing since sliced beer, but I have no way of knowing."

Monique Haas, vice president of family-owned Hutzler Manufacturing Co., in Canaan, Conn., said when the design team came up with the 571, she wondered whether the world needed another way to cut bananas. She came around after her children test-drove the $3.59 device. It hasn't hurt that the wiseguy reviews have boosted Hutzler's sales among wiseguys.

The sharpest-edged consumer sarcasm seems reserved for the thin-barreled BIC Cristal For Her Ball Pens.

"The delicate shape and pretty pastel colors make it perfect for writing recipe cards, checks to my psychologist (I'm seeing him for a case of the hysterics), and tracking my monthly cycle," wrote one reviewer. "Obviously, I don't use it for vulgar endeavors like math or filling out a voter application, but BIC Cristal for Her is a lovely little writing utensil all the same. Ask your husband for some extra pocket money so you can buy one today!"

A package of 16 sells for $13.12.

"We continue to be intrigued by the conversation that surrounds the BIC for Her line and are always interested in hearing consumer feedback about our products," said BIC USA spokeswoman Jill Johnson.

WORK

Cupids-for-Hire

JENNIFER LEVITZ

Cort Johnson

BOSTON—Cort Johnson, 27 years old, is an affable guy who's skilled at promoting his company—a mobile-application start-up he co-founded. But when it comes to socializing, especially with women, he tends to clam up.

"I'd like to be romantic," he sighs. "But how?"

For Mr. Johnson and many others, the answer is "hire a coach."

Hoping to meet some prospects at a holiday party in December, Mr. Johnson enlisted Thomas Edwards, who runs a service called "The Professional Wingman." For a fee of $125, Mr. Edwards accompanied Mr. Johnson to the event and posed as his good pal. As they negotiated the crowd, the wingman alerted his charge to flirtatious types and helped make seamless introductions.

"I love that," said Mr. Johnson.

As romantics grow weary of the digital dating game, so-called wingman and wingwoman services are taking them back in time. Such outfits, which popped up in cities like Boston and New York as long as eight years ago, are promoting the old-fashioned tete-a-tete. They're gaining traction at a time when Internet dating sites are attracting fewer visitors.

Susan Baxter, founder of "Hire a Boston Wingwoman," says she launched her business specifically because her friends were fatigued by online dating. She sensed a good niche.

"You go to meet [the person] and realize their picture was taken 10 years ago and that they are not who you thought," says Ms. Baxter, 32 years old. Paired with a confident wingwoman, her customers "can see prospective partners right away, and know right then and there if there is chemistry."

Ms. Baxter, whose fees start at $130, insists that clients who go out with a pro have better odds of success than those who troll with an untrained male buddy. Often, the friend "says stupid stuff, like 'my friend thinks you're hot,'" she says.

The service's slogan: "We're better at hitting on women than you are."

While online dating sites have changed the dance of romance, academic researchers have been skeptical about sites' purported "success" (code word for marriage) rates. And the Federal Bureau of Investigation, which handles Internet crimes, says it receives thousands of complaints annually from people who get scammed by shady suitors. In an ongoing lawsuit filed in federal court in Dallas a year ago, several Match.com customers sued the company, saying that many of its profiles are phony or are linked to inactive members.

A spokeswoman for Match.com calls the lawsuit "frivolous."

The wingman has been on the dating scene since the days of Shakespeare, when Romeo's closest pal Mercutio helps him to forget a girlfriend by taking him to a masked ball at Lord Capulet's estate to meet other women (in the end, that didn't go well). More recently, the wingman has been celebrated in movies like "Hitch," a 2005 comedy starring Will Smith as a professional Cupid.

Most services say they tend to focus on male clients, the theory being that men need more help since women often go out in groups, making it harder for a lone guy to break in. But the wings-for-hire say they do sometimes fly with female clients, too.

Josh Mitchell, 27, started his Indianapolis wingwoman service, "Miss Pivot," last year after attending an event for young entrepreneurs. Romance aside, there was something else that convinced him he had a winning concept. No one, he says, seems to know how to have a face-to-face conversation anymore. "A lot of social skills you used to pick up watching your parents, but now everyone is busy watching stuff online or playing videogames online," he says.

Mr. Mitchell now runs Miss Pivot with a team of five friends, including a "head coach," plus eight freelance "pivots" for hire at $45 to $65 an hour.

Not everyone is cut out for the matchmaking work. "We don't want someone with a really annoying voice," says Mr. Mitchell. Another no-no: overly emotional types. "They tend to think love is very magical while we think there is a science behind it," he says.

For the dates, the pivots generally stay away from night-clubs, and go to bookstores, coffee shops or pubs where the tables are high. "Sitting on stools brings everyone up to the same level," says Mr. Mitchell.

At the Boston holiday party called "Ugly Sweater Night," Mr. Johnson had slipped in with his wingman. Revelers, dressed in blinking Christmas sweaters, sipped bottles of beer and shimmied to the rap song "Bust a Move."

Mr. Johnson, wearing a Santa hat, scanned the room and homed in on a blonde woman in reindeer ears dancing with two friends. "She looks fun," he told his wingman.

"I'll go in," Mr. Edwards replied.

Moving quickly, he saw that one of the women had a camera and asked if he could take the group's picture.

Giggling, they huddled together. But when a few people behind them tried to squeeze into the picture, the women stopped posing and looked annoyed.

In their pre-event strategy session, Mr. Edwards had determined that Mr. Johnson is inclusive and fun-loving and needs the same in a partner. He backed away and shook his head at Mr. Johnson, signaling that the young woman wasn't worth pursuing.

"I'm an extension of Cort. If that turned me off, it will definitely turn Cort off," said Mr. Edwards.

Mr. Johnson moved through the crowd and talked to several women with Mr. Edwards by his side. "Thomas is a confidence builder," he said.

When a woman complimented Mr. Edwards's fuzzy white sweater, he put an arm around his client and said, "It would look much better on him."

In their strategy session, they had looked at "sticking points" that were keeping Mr. Johnson from romance. "If he likes someone, he doesn't make it clear he's interested," Mr. Edwards said.

But near midnight came Mr. Johnson's breakthrough. A woman he had talked to earlier, and had liked, sat in a chair pointed away from her table.

He walked over and sat on her lap. Mr. Edwards stared, astonished. The woman's hand went up and around Mr. Johnson's shoulder.

"I love it!" Mr. Edwards said. "I knew Cort had this in him." A short while later, Mr. Johnson reported back to his tutor, grinning, and with the woman's phone number.

Though he was a friend for hire, Mr. Edwards's enthusiasm seemed real when he slapped Mr. Johnson's back and shouted, "Good job!"

Wingman Meets His Match

JENNIFER LEVITZ

Thomas Edwards said "The Professional Wingman" business is up to nearly 500 clients, most of them people who want to meet a life partner. "They are pretty successful and have most of their stuff together but it's just the one thing that is missing," he said. Two people he has coached have gotten married, five are engaged, and another has a baby on the way, he said. Mr. Edwards himself is engaged to a female dating coach who teaches people how to flirt. He did not use a wingman to meet her, but did take his own advice while courting her. "At this point I've seen it all. I do know most of the things not to do," he said.

Cort Johnson, now 28, said he is happily in a relationship with a woman he met through a co-worker. He said he remains friends with Mr. Edwards, and that his time with the professional wingman mainly helped Mr. Johnson to become more at ease talking to potential dates. "I gained confidence as a result of that," he said.

The lawsuit filed in federal court in Dallas against Match.com by several customers was dismissed in October 2012, but the plaintiffs have appealed.

Clawing Their Way to the Top

KATHERINE ROSMAN

Grumpy Cat

Some celebrities simply cannot be pleased. Just ask Ben Lashes, a talent manager in Los Angeles. This week, he landed a major motion-picture deal for a client who nine months ago was an unknown living in Morristown, Ariz., population 227.

When he told his client that she was heading to Hollywood, she looked bored. "She hates movies," says Mr. Lashes of his client, Grumpy Cat, a cat with a mouth puckered into a frown whose viral photos have ricocheted around the Internet.

Mr. Lashes, whose legal name is Benjamin Clark and who is 34 years old, is an agent for Internet cats. When an ironic photograph of a feline becomes Internet famous, Mr. Lashes contacts the pet owner and offers to help strategize ways to prolong, protect and monetize. He says he operates with this question in mind: "What would Walt Disney do if he created Mickey Mouse and it went viral on YouTube?"

Grumpy Cat, the Arizona sourpuss, is Mr. Lashes's star client. The cat is having a mini-Mickey moment.

Last September, Bryan Bundesen, 34, a cable technician

from Galion, Ohio, was visiting his sister Tabatha in Arizona. He snapped a photo of her cat, a mixed breed whose real name is Tardar Sauce. (Ms. Bundesen, who works as a waitress at a Red Lobster, says her daughter thought the cat's fur was the color of tartar sauce, but misspelled it.) Mr. Bundesen posted the picture on the website Reddit. People thought it was funny. Many began to overlay the photo with sentences expressing what they imagined to be the cat's irritation with humans: "I thought I could not be more disappointed . . . you proved me wrong," reads one of thousands. "There are two kinds of people in this world . . . and I don't like them," says another.

Within weeks, photos and videos of the cat had been shared and posted to social-media sites millions of times.

Mr. Lashes became the cat's representative in October. He says he is trying to help the Bundesens capitalize on the cat's fame without overexposing it. This week, Mr. Lashes helped negotiate the sale of a film option based on Grumpy Cat's persona to Broken Road Productions, the production company responsible for Adam Sandler's 2011 vehicle "Jack and Jill." Terms of the one-picture deal weren't disclosed.

This week, Grumpy Cat is coming to New York to promote the forthcoming Chronicle Books release, "Grumpy Cat: A Grumpy Book: Disgruntled Tips and Activities Designed to Put a Frown on Your Face" at BookExpo America, the publishing industry convention.

Mr. Lashes also has forged a deal with Grenade Beverage LLC to create and distribute a line of Grumpy Cat coffee-in-cans and bottled beverages. Excluding the movie deal, the Bundesens have earned a low-six-figure sum off the cat thus far, Mr. Bundesen says. Mr. Lashes's take is about 20%, clients say. (Mr. Lashes declined to comment on financial arrangements.)

"He is really good at helping us not get taken advantage of," Mr. Bundesen says of Mr. Lashes.

Mr. Lashes grew up in Spokane, Wash. After a year of college, he dropped out in 2000 to pursue his dream of becoming a professional musician. He fronted a band and worked in talent scouting for an independent label.

In 2010, he heard from Charlie Schmidt, an old friend of his father's and a multimedia artist in Spokane. Back in 1985, Mr. Schmidt told Mr. Lashes, he had dressed his now deceased cat, Fatso, in a blue T-shirt, sat him at a keyboard and manipulated the cat such that it played a song Mr. Schmidt wrote. Mr. Schmidt had recently posted the old video on YouTube. Keyboard Cat was blowing up.

Mr. Lashes started helping his family friend, creating a social-media strategy to fan the cat's grass-roots popularity. He told Mr. Schmidt to adopt a new cat and make more videos. Then came the licensing deals with T-shirt, toy and novelty gift companies. Soon, Mr. Lashes was making deals for the cat to appear in marketing and ad campaigns. In all, Mr. Schmidt says he has made nearly $300,000 from Keyboard Cat deals Mr. Lashes has arranged.

Mr. Lashes now lives in West Hollywood, Calif., where he works out of his one-bedroom condo. His newest client is Princess Monster Truck, a cat with an underbite. "When it comes to cats, Ben knows who is going to be big," says Christopher Torres, a client of Mr. Lashes and the creator of Nyan Cat, a digital, square-shaped feline. Mr. Lashes also represents other photographs, images, sayings or ideas that spread online and become cultural inside jokes.

Mr. Lashes says he tries to help his clients protect their brands as well.

Last month, Messrs. Torres and Schmidt filed a lawsuit with the U.S. District Court in the central district of California. They allege that 5th Cell and Warner Bros.— respectively the developer and publisher of the Scribblenauts franchise of videogames—have infringed on the copyright and trademark right of Keyboard Cat and Nyan Cat, by including the characters in Scribblenauts games.

"If you're a big corporation and you normally pay for the use of these things, we will come after you," says Kia Kamran, an attorney who works with Mr. Lashes on his clients' transaction matters and who also represents the intellectual property rights of the tattoo on former boxer Mike Tyson's face.

A spokeswoman for Warner Bros. Interactive Entertainment declined to comment. 5th Cell didn't respond to requests for comment.

Mr. Lashes says he is driven by a desire to "protect the

little guy" but also to have fun. At the South by Southwest tech convention in Austin, Texas, in March, he arranged a paid-appearance deal for Grumpy Cat from the website Mashable. For two-hour stretches over three days, the cat lay on a cushioned pedestal in Mashable's tent and conventioneers waited in line for hours to have their photo taken with the nonplused puss.

The logistics weren't that complicated to work through—Grumpy Cat was already scheduled to be in Austin to tape a celebrity edition of an online game show, "Will Kitty Play With It?"

As part of the travel expenses covered by Friskies, the cat-food brand that sponsors the game show, Mr. Bundesen says he chauffeured Grumpy Cat around Austin in a black BMW X5, with tinted windows. When they left the final day of the Mashable appearance, he says the car was swamped by 40 to 50 people taking photos of the cat through the car windows. "It was like the paparazzi," he says.

Update

Grumpy Cat Is Top Dog at Show

JO PIAZZA

The breakout star of Friday's BookExpo America at the Javits Center wasn't the actor Jim Carrey, former First Lady contender Ann Romney, or NBA all-time leading scorer Kareem Abdul-Jabbar. It was none other than meme sensation Grumpy Cat, who drew a line of hundreds of fans, some of whom waited more than two hours just to take a photograph with the cantankerous feline.

"There are 10,000 librarians here and just one cat. Of course the line is this long. This is the most exciting thing I have done all day," said Connecticut librarian Casey Caplante. "I'm going to be a grumpy librarian by the time I finally get to see the cat."

The line to meet the Internet sensation started at 1:15 p.m., almost two hours before the cat was due to make her appearance. Just 15 minutes into the event, the crowd was so anxious to get close to Grumpy Cat that the BEA organizers called for two extra security guards to maintain the peace.

Grumpy Cat, whose real name is Tardar Sauce, managed to sleep through most of her event, waking only when her owner, Tabatha Bundesen, picked her up from her plush bed to make her famously grumpy face, a trait caused by feline dwarfism.

"People in line keep telling us she is their spirit animal," explained Sarah Malarkey, the Executive Editorial Director of Chronicle Books, the imprint that will publish "Grumpy Cat: A Grumpy Book" in the fall.

Chronicle was loath to reveal where the famous cat and her handlers were staying while in the city. "We really can't reveal that. Last time she was in New York someone broke down crying when they saw her," Ms. Malarkey said.

Stand-Up Jobs

RACHEL EMMA SILVERMAN

Atomic Object, a Grand Rapids, Mich., software-development firm, holds company meetings first thing in the morning.

Employees follow strict rules: Attendance is mandatory, nonwork chitchat is kept to a minimum and, above all, everyone has to stand up.

Stand-up meetings are part of a fast-moving tech culture in which sitting has become synonymous with sloth. The object is to eliminate long-winded confabs where participants pontificate, play Angry Birds on their cellphones or tune out.

Atomic Object even frowns upon tables during meetings. "They make it too easy to lean or rest laptops," explains Michael Marsiglia, vice president. At the end of the meetings, which rarely last more than five minutes, employees typically do a quick stretch and then "go on with their day," he says.

Holding meetings standing up isn't new. Some military leaders did it during World War I, according to Allen Bluedorn, a business professor at the University of Missouri. A number of companies have adopted stand-up meetings over the years. Mr. Bluedorn did a study back in 1998 that found that standing meetings were about a third shorter than sitting meetings and the quality of decision-making was about the same.

The current wave of stand-up meetings is being fueled by the growing use of "Agile," an approach to software development, crystallized in a manifesto published by 17 software professionals in 2001. The method calls for compressing development projects into short pieces. It also involves daily stand-up meetings where participants are supposed to quickly update their peers with three things: What they have done since yesterday's meeting; what they are doing today; and any obstacles that stand in the way of getting work done.

If employees are late to this meeting, often called a "daily scrum," they sometimes must sing a song like "I'm a Little Teapot," do a lap around the office building or pay a small fine, says Mike Cohn, president of Mountain Goat Software, Lafayette, Colo., an Agile consultant and trainer. If someone is rambling on for too long, an employee may hold up a rubber rat indicating it is time to move on. Companies make exceptions to their no-sitting rules if a worker is sick, injured or pregnant—but usually not for workers outside the office telecommuting on Skype.

One Microsoft Corp. development group holds daily meetings in which participants toss around a rubber chicken named Ralph to determine who gets to speak next, says group member Aaron Bjork.

As Agile has become more widely adopted, stand-ups have spread along with it. VersionOne, which makes Agile-development software, polled 6,042 tech employees around the world in a 2011 survey and found that 78% held daily stand-up meetings.

Office outfitters are responding by designing work spaces with standing sessions in mind. Furniture maker Steelcase Inc.'s Turnstone division, for example, recently introduced the "Big Table," a large standing-height table designed for quick meetings.

Mitch Lacey, a Bellevue, Wash., tech consultant and a former Microsoft employee, says that some of his former colleagues used to hold stand-ups in an unheated stairwell to keep meetings brief.

Holding meetings before lunch also speeds things up. Mark Tonkelowitz, an engineering manager for Facebook Inc.'s News Feed feature, holds 15-minute stand-ups at noon, sharp. The proximity to lunch serves "as motivation to keep updates short," he says.

Sometimes people cheat a bit. "We have some very good slouchers and leaners," says T.A. McCann, founder of Gist, a Seattle contact-organization tool acquired last year by Research In Motion, which holds a 10 a.m. stand-up three days a week.

Obie Fernandez, founder of Hashrocket, a Jacksonville, Fla., software design firm, says his team passes around a 10-pound medicine ball during stand-ups. For newcomers unaware of the practice, "it's pretty mean," he says, "but really the main thing you want is to avoid people pontificating."

Participants frown upon late arrivals, and some data-obsessed engineers have even computed the costs of tardiness. Ian Witucki, a program manager at software firm Adobe Systems Inc., calculated the cumulative cost over the course of a typical 18-month product release cycle of starting the stand-up just a little bit late every day.

The total—about six weeks of work for two employees—equaled the amount of time the firm could spend building one major feature on each product, he says.

Soon after, the team imposed a $1 fine for latecomers. Now staffers run down the hall to make it on time, says Mr. Witucki.

Jason Yip, a principal consultant at ThoughtWorks in Sydney, Australia, plays music such as Bob Marley's "Get Up, Stand Up," to round up colleagues. "It acts like a Pavlovian bell," he says.

Meanwhile, the Starr Conspiracy, a Fort Worth, Texas, advertising, marketing and branding agency, signals its daily stand-up—which it calls "the huddle"—with a few bars of the song, "Whoomp! (There It Is)," says partner Steve Smith.

"I'll be at a football game, hear the song and all of a sudden I have the urge to huddle up," says Mr. Smith.

Steelcase's Turnstone unit, which has been doing stand-up meetings for about a decade, for years played Johnny Cash's "Ring of Fire," to begin meetings. It recently switched to Elvis's "A Little Less Conversation"—a reminder to keep meetings brief, says general manager Kevin Kuske.

There are occasions when even a stand-up takes too much time.

At Freshbooks.com, a Toronto-based company that makes online accounting software, teams try to do daily 10 a.m. stand-ups. But on days when everyone is too swamped to gather around the company Ping-Pong table, team members will shout out their status updates from their desks, which are arranged in a circle.

They call those meetings "sit-downs."

Fur Flies

ANN ZIMMERMAN

Time was, all dog groomers had to offer was a bath, a trim and maybe a perky bow for that pampered toy poodle. Today, customers pay to have their dogs—and even cats—dyed the colors of their favorite football teams, tinted orange and streaked black to resemble tigers, or given multicolor mohawks.

For the most ambitious professionals, so-called creative grooming has also become a sport, with a dozen contests around the country each year. Contestants have dyed and clipped dogs to resemble lions, cows, lizards, dolphins and, in one case, a large garden snail.

The events are so intense that a few years ago they spawned a brief reality TV series—"Extreme Poodles." And the entries have only gotten more elaborate: Instead of turning a dog into a leopard, now a groomer will turn his coat into a jungle tableau, including vines, toucans and an iguana.

Animal rights groups aren't amused—but even some passionate creative groomers worry that things have gone too far.

Amy Brown once spent a year turning her dog Xerxes into a "zombie poodle" for a children's hospital fundraiser in Birmingham, Ala. Carved and tinted to look like a skeleton, the dog's coat also featured gray and green tufts and highlights.

Ms. Brown now devotes much of her time leading a group of 300 groomers who are pushing to ban the use of hair bleach and other potentially caustic chemicals in creative grooming. She and members of her group, the National Association of Professional Creative Groomers, say that the chemicals can irritate a dog's skin and mucous membranes, though she can't produce documentation of an animal that has been injured. The American Kennel Club prohibits the use of dyes of any kind on dogs entered in its sanctioned shows.

"It's like using steroids or throwing points in a game. It's not good for your sport," says Ms. Brown, who owns 14 dogs and runs a grooming salon in Childersburg, Ala.

Her campaign upset rivals who don't think there is anything wrong with using dyes that contain a bleaching agent. These groomers, many of them award winners, recently formed their own group, the Creative Groomers Association.

President Lori Craig says banning bleach products from competition is an overreaction. "It's hurting the industry and dividing people," says Ms. Craig, who runs a grooming salon in Moore, Okla.

But Ms. Brown's anti-bleach crusade seems to be having an effect. Her organization persuaded the United Show Managers Alliance, which produces three contests a year, to ban most bleach except for small amounts to remove stains from a dog's coat.

The biggest contest and trade show company, Barkleigh Productions, recently responded. Just in time for the company's biggest event, the Groom Expo in Hershey, Pa., Barkleigh changed its rules to allow only 15% of an animal's body to be bleached.

For the rest of the dog, groomers could use non-peroxide-based dyes instead.

The president of Barkleigh, Todd Shelly, acknowledges the rift in the industry. "Frankly I think it is two groups of groomers who don't like each other," says Mr. Shelly. "It's like high school."

Jerry Schinberg, a retired groomer from Des Plaines, Ill., a suburb northwest of Chicago, is largely credited with creating creative grooming in 1980 when he decided to spice up a trade show he produced. He says he doesn't know if bleach causes problems or not, and for that reason he thinks it shouldn't be used.

As for the divisions the debate has caused, he says, the two factions will make the industry better.

"It's like politics," Mr. Schinberg says. "When the two extremes meet in the middle, it works better."

The controversy seeped into the creative groomer contest last Sunday, which capped the three-day pet-products trade fair. A record 5,000 people checked out booths hawking products such as Pup Feathers, decorative plumes that can be attached to a dog's fur like hair extensions. Some visitors brought their dogs along, including some tiny ones that rode in strollers. Many people brought their children, at least one of whom was on a leash.

The high point, as usual, was the contest, at which more than a dozen groomers spent three hours in front of an audience airbrushing, stenciling and shearing their dogs as they vied for a $2,500 grand prize and the chance to be on the cover of Barkleigh's *Groomer to Groomer* magazine.

Ms. Brown boycotted the competition, because she said Barkleigh's contest rules don't go far enough to protect dogs. But Justine Cosley, a cat groomer from Pittsburgh, entered although she is an active member of Ms. Brown's association.

"Some of our members say to compete here is to condone, but I think I need to get up there and set a good example," she says. Ms. Cosley spent the last four months dying different swatches of her poodle pink, lime green, brown and black, sections that would turn into a flamingo, macaw and palm tree.

Ms. Cosley didn't win.

Nor did Ms. Craig, who runs the bleach-tolerant group. She turned her white standard poodle, Falcore, into a replica of a panda, with a geisha carved into his fur on one side and a cherry blossom tree on the other.

Both were eclipsed by Cindy Oliver of Cleveland, Ohio, who won first place for a fantasia on the theme of Pinocchio.

The People's Choice Award, chosen by how loud the audience clapped, went to Jean Honsinger from Youngstown, Ohio, who dyed her dog green and turned him into Yoda from Star Wars, with an Ewok carved into his hindquarters.

But the rift was never far from groomers' minds. Cat Opson from Dana Point, Calif., told the judges that "turmoil in the creative grooming industry" inspired her design on a poodle featuring Big Bird and Elmo from *Sesame Street*.

"I want us to get along like we are kindergartners," Ms. Opson said.

Update

After the Storm

ANN ZIMMERMAN

Lori Craig's salon, Doggie Styles, was buffeted twice by tornados that ripped through her hometown of Moore, Okla., in May.

The first twister damaged the salon's roof. The second flooded the shop and ripped the roof off. She was closed for two weeks.

In the meantime, she organized a group of fellow groomers to bathe and style dogs that had been displaced during the tornado and available for adoption.

Her shop is back in business and Ms. Craig continues to compete in creative grooming contests.

When Mom Goes Viral

JAMES R. HAGERTY

Marilyn Hagerty

S ome people pursue celebrity. Others stumble into it as they are rushing off to bridge club.

My 85-year-old mom, Marilyn Hagerty, a newspaper columnist, is in the latter category. When she wrote a review of the new Olive Garden restaurant in Grand Forks, N.D., last week, she wasn't expecting anyone other than her thousands of loyal readers in North Dakota and northwestern Minnesota to take note. She didn't worry about how her story would play on Gawker, partly because she had never heard of Gawker.

She's too busy to bother with blogs, Facebook or Twitter. She writes five articles a week for the *Grand Forks Herald*. Her specialties include local personalities, history and, yes, restaurants of high and low repute. Those whom she dubs in her column as "cheerful person of the week" consider it a high honor. She also cleans and maintains her house, cares for an unreliable dachshund, visits her eight grandchildren and volunteers at church.

Bloggers happened on her review of the Olive Garden, where she found the portions generous and the decor "impressive." Some wrote clever notes suggesting there might be some sort of irony in writing an unironic review about a chain restaurant like Olive Garden. Others, including media and news websites Gawker and Huffington Post, chimed in. Soon news hounds from Minneapolis, New York and even Fargo were calling Mom and demanding interviews. Basically, they wanted to know whether she was for real and how she felt about being mocked all over the Internet.

She felt fine about it. But she didn't care to scroll through the thousands of Twitter and Facebook comments on her writing style. "I'm working on my Sunday column and I'm going to play bridge this afternoon," she explained, "so I don't have time to read all this crap." She didn't apologize for writing about a restaurant where many people like to eat. Her poise under fire endeared her to people who do read all that. Strangers started sending me emails about how much they loved my mom.

Her phone line was tied up, so I emailed her: "You've gone viral!"

She replied: "Could you tell me what viral means?"

Though she may not be hip to social media, Mom was always ready with the right quip. I remember a time when she and my father were posing for a portrait. The photographer asked Dad to raise his chin a bit. "Which one?" Mom deadpanned.

After 65 years of writing and editing for newspapers in both of the Dakotas, she didn't need to worry about leaving a mark on the world. She had already done that.

More than a decade ago, she mused in one of her columns that it would be nice to have something named after her. It wouldn't have to be a grand building or a stadium, she wrote. A sewage-pumping station would do. The mayor of Grand Forks eventually complied. Visitors to the town will note the Marilyn Hagerty sewage facility, with a suitably engraved plaque in her honor, on Belmont Road.

Despite having secured her reputation for posterity, Mom retains her work ethic. When she takes a vacation, it is only after writing enough articles in advance to fill her daily space. She pays her own way at restaurants, rather than submitting expenses, so no one can say she does reviews just to get free meals. When she was successfully treated for breast cancer two years ago, she used the occasion to write a review of the hospital's food. It was right up there with the cuisine at Olive Garden.

My mom has her own style of reviewing restaurants: She doesn't like to say anything bad about the food. Her regular readers read between the lines. If she writes more about the decor than the food, you might want to eat somewhere else.

Her Olive Garden review was actually mixed. She said the "chicken Alfredo ($10.95) was warm and comforting on a cold day." She also noted that the restaurant is "fashioned in Tuscan farmhouse style with a welcoming entryway."

"As I ate," Mom wrote, "I noticed the vases and planters with permanent flower displays on the ledges. There are several dining areas with arched doorways. And there is a fireplace that adds warmth to the decor."

A spokesman for owner Darden Restaurants Inc. said Olive Garden is a "beloved brand" and "proud of the food they produce."

Mom doesn't consider herself a food critic. She lives in a college town with its share of local wiseguys. She knows a thing or two about snide comments and condescension. As she told one interviewer, "I don't have time to sit here and twit over whether some self-styled food expert likes, or does not like, my column."

Her restaurant reviews, after all, are only a sideline. She's more at home writing about people.

One of her best stories, in my view, was a 1974 profile of a bachelor farmer, Magnus Skytland, who lived quite happily without electricity. He read by the light of a kerosene lamp and sometimes serenaded himself on his violin. He showed my mom his favorite horse, Sally, named after a former girlfriend. "I've had three horses named Sally," he said.

The story about Sally is in a book of Mom's old columns, "Echoes," listed on Amazon as being worth $16 new or $15.50 used. Given the fleeting nature of Internet celebrity, this might be a good time to cash in. Still, I'm hanging on to my copy.

The only downside of the world's belated discovery of my mom is that she is too busy being interviewed on national television to play online Scrabble with me.

Mom, if you ever get time to read this, it's your move.

Update

Mom's Fame Grows
Beyond Internet

JAMES R. HAGERTY

My mom's fame has lasted longer than any of us expected. She appeared on the television show "Top Chef" in 2012, and chef Anthony Bourdain's Ecco imprint is due to publish a book of her columns, *Grand Forks: A History of American Dining in 100 Reviews*, in August 2013.

Most things haven't changed: She still writes five articles a week for the *Grand Forks Herald*, and she still mows her lawn, cleans up after her unruly dachshund and finds time for bridge.

The Dirt on Dirty Jokes

BARRY NEWMAN

Jeff Lawrence

NEW YORK—Aspiring stand-up comedians often think that making people laugh requires a foul mouth. Could be, but most of them won't earn a cent at it if they can't clean up their acts.

As Jeff Lawrence told a group of somber would-be comics one evening: "If you have a great set and you don't curse, nobody ever leaves going, 'That guy was great, too bad he didn't curse.'"

"Just saying the word [something] doesn't make people laugh," he added unprintably. "So don't say it, for [something's] sake!"

Mr. Lawrence is a fortyish, gay Jewish comic who hasn't quite sworn off swearing himself. He runs a comedy school, called Laughing Buddha, out of a comedy club in Manhattan. After lecturing his class on the importance of immaculate auditions for bookers and agents, he called his students to the stage to run through their material.

First up was David Friedlander, a young man in khakis and a button-down shirt who started with a story about his efforts to lose weight and went on to a vivid anecdote involving genitalia.

"David," Mr. Lawrence said when he was done, "you aren't fat. To do fat jokes, you got to be fat." Mr. Friedlander looked down at his stomach. "And you've got a [something] joke and a [something worse] joke," Mr. Lawrence continued. "Too much of a risk there. You just need more stage time. Good stuff, David. Let him hear it!"

The students clapped.

Stand-up wouldn't be stand-up if comics didn't test limits, so it is natural for newcomers to idolize iconoclasts. But comics rarely know they have reached a limit until they have crossed it. With YouTube as a megaphone, several have crossed it lately, telling jokes on such jovial topics as rape and mass murder. Not many comedy bookers were amused. They already know dirt doesn't pay well.

"Dirty comics get famous fast, clean comics make more money," says Bobby Gonzo, a longtime booker for 300 "squeaky clean to medium clean" rooms around the country. "I don't believe in 'hurt comedy,'" he says. "Not raunchy. Not disgusting. Not hurtful."

Patrick Milligan, founder of a New York management outfit called "Cringe Humor," feels Mr. Gonzo's pain, reluctantly.

"Nobody can make a joke about anything anymore," he says. "You talk about a dog drowning and it's, 'Oh, my dog drowned. I'm going to blog about it.' Next thing you know, a comedian's apologizing."

Mr. Milligan coaxes comics to write "a clean set to carry them through the business," and to "address the vile stuff without making it hate speech." Stars like Chris Rock and Louis C.K. still make 'em cringe on major tours and late-night cable; journeymen who don't like watching their tongues have to settle for dives like the ones in Times Square.

The 9 p.m. show at the Broadway Comedy Club one Thursday began with a limbo act. Then came four comics who told jokes about Viagra, North Dakota, cocaine, Italians and a spectrum of reproductive and emunctory functions. Steve Marshall closed with: "I know you loved this because you're sick [somethings]! Good night, everybody!"

As the audience left, Teresa Sales, an immigrant from Serbia, offered a review. "I liked the limbo girls," she said. "If they had a fire-eater it would have been cool."

Big-city clubs have a dirty secret: Even the pros earn only a few hundred dollars a set, if that. Stand-up's steady money is at colleges, festivals, churches and—for $10,000 a pop—in the spotless dinners, trade shows and pep talks put on by corporations.

"If you're OK for corporate, you're OK for family, OK for cruise ships," says Suzy Yengo, who owns Catch A Rising Star, a string of clubs dating back to 1972. And OK for parks on summer afternoons.

Suzette Simon produces "Laughter in the Park," a stand-up series funded by New York City and several supermarkets. "It's got to be clean," says Ms. Simon. "I respect freedom of speech, but I need permits. Anyhow, dirt doesn't work in the sunshine."

On a sunny Sunday in Central Park, Myq Kaplan scanned the crowd and opened with: "You guys are my demographic, which is people who know the word 'demographic.'" Comics followed with jokes about animals, smoking, the recession. Phoebe Robinson did a camping joke and a bit about having a white boyfriend. Then she said:

"I'm looking for a family-friendly joke to close on. It's tough. You can't talk about penises." Some people snickered. "You guys have been fantastic!" said Ms. Robinson. The applause was polite.

Working clean, for sure, is tougher than overworking race, sex and obscenity. Sometimes, it is exhilarating, too.

"Clean can be edgy," says comedian Vanessa Hollingshead, who made her maiden cruise-ship voyage last year. "I didn't swear once and they still laughed! Wow, I must have been angry. What a great feeling—to be really mad and really clean."

It is the feeling Mr. Lawrence was hoping to get across to his comedy class as he invited his students to the stage: a mortician, an Orthodox Jew, an Indian Catholic, a woman getting divorced. They were paying $50 apiece for one session on the art of auditioning.

"Some of these people don't even understand what clean is," Mr. Lawrence whispered before Jeffrey Paul approached the microphone.

"I used to work in law enforcement," Mr. Paul began. "I was stabbed on the job. I didn't like the feeling of getting stabbed on the job. The feeling of not getting stabbed? I like that better."

He got a laugh. He then reported an observation he had made in the shower involving his nether reaches. Nobody laughed at that.

"I don't want to hear about your [somethings]," Mr. Lawrence cut in. "I don't want to hear about anybody's [somethings]." Mr. Paul took notes. "But you were stabbed? Stabbed on the job?"

"If you were a fugitive, I went out and got you," said Mr. Paul. One of the students piped up: "Sounds like a bounty hunter."

"Exactly," Mr. Lawrence said. "Instead of giving us your life as a bounty hunter, you're talking about your [somethings]."

"I was stabbed with a Phillips screwdriver," Mr. Paul said, and Mr. Lawrence beamed. "Yes! Yes! Now you've got a little Phillips mark. People think it's a tattoo of a starfish. Run with it! Great stabbing joke! Everybody, let's hear it for Jeff Paul!"

The students put down their pens and gave him a hand.

Dogfight at the Pentagon

JULIAN E. BARNES

Sgt. Chesty XIII

WASHINGTON—The Marines won't say it out loud, but everyone knows that Cpl. Chesty got promoted to sergeant this summer not for being a good Marine, but for his in-your-muzzle confrontation with the top dog in the Pentagon.

Just two weeks before his promotion, the Marine Corps mascot, an English bulldog formally known as Chesty XIII, had a run-in with Bravo, Defense Secretary Leon Panetta's golden retriever. Chesty, usually known for happily mugging for photos with kids, revealed his inner grunt when he spotted the larger dog at the conclusion of a pomp-filled military parade held in honor of the Pentagon chief. Chesty growled, barked and ignored his choke-chain of command as he went nose-to-nose with Bravo.

As Chesty's growl erupted into an angry bark, an officer urgently whispered in the ear of his handler, Sgt. Chris Harris: "Keep the leash tight."

That kind of breach of decorum at the headquarters barracks, where the top generals and their wives reside, could have been career-ending for most Marines.

Chesty weathered the controversy and came out of it with a new stripe on his uniform.

Privately, some wives of senior Marine officers, more focused on politeness than doggedness, let it be known they didn't approve of the promotion. A whispering campaign against Chesty reached the ears of Col. Paul Montanus, barracks commander. Some said Chesty was getting too fat. Some senior wives wanted Chesty relieved of duty in favor of a more pliable bulldog private serving in another unit.

Other senior Marines worried about the message promoting Chesty might send. In military chain of command, Bravo is second only to Bo Obama, the president's hypoallergenic Portuguese water dog. The Constitution puts the military under civilian control, and some senior officers thought promoting Chesty might appear insubordinate.

"The standards in the barracks had lowered," said one senior Marine officer. "The dog didn't really deserve it."

Col. Montanus, who had the dog's fate in his hands, acknowledges that Chesty was wrong to shove his short snout in Bravo's face. "There absolutely was a protocol break," he said. "We don't bark at guests, whether they are human or the canine variety."

But, the colonel said, much of the opposition was baseless. A barracks spokesman says senior Marine wives love and support the current Chesty. And at 54 pounds, Chesty fits nicely in the dress blues he was issued as a younger dog, thanks to being served half the daily kibble ration of his chunky predecessors.

Nevertheless, in a speech at Chesty's June promotion ceremony, Col. Montanus acknowledged the decision was "touch and go."

"There are some Marines that are destined to be sergeant," he said. "Then there are some whose conduct is . . . questionable. Chesty is one of those Marines."

Col. Montanus said he had considered formally punishing Chesty for "disrespect to a superior commissioned dog."

It is true that "Chesty made threatening gestures," he said. "But we decided the body of work for Chesty was enough he rated becoming a sergeant."

Left unspoken: The very act that made Chesty's promotion controversial also made it more likely.

Immediately after the parade in honor of Mr. Panetta it became clear that going muzzle-to-muzzle with the 75-pound golden retriever was going to enhance Chesty's reputation in the ranks.

While Mr. Panetta was present, the top Marines displayed embarrassed grins and laughed nervously. But after the boss left, the high-fives and atta-boys broke out. Far from being denied his traditional post-parade Milk-Bone, the bulldog found himself the object of warrior admiration. Even Gen. James Amos, the Marine commandant, approached Chesty and said, "Good job."

There is a reason the Corps has a bulldog for a mascot and that he is named after the famously gutsy Marine Lt. Gen. Lewis "Chesty" Puller. Even within a service that values discipline, there is a certain mystique about a Marine who's willing to poke a paw in the eye of power—particularly in defense of the homeland, or kennel.

Col. Montanus's successor as barracks commander, Col. Christian Cabaniss, made plain the current Chesty had only grown in his estimation.

"Chesty embodies Gen. [James] Mattis's saying about the Marines: 'No better friend, no worse enemy,'" Col. Cabaniss said. "Chesty's great. He is great with kids. But if you are impolite to him, if you are wrong, that is when he will defend himself."

Like Chesty, Gen. Mattis has risen through the ranks despite the occasional public display of machismo—comments such as "Be polite, be professional, but have a plan to kill everybody you meet"—that has raised eyebrows with civilians.

Gen. Mattis, who oversees operations in the Middle East and Afghanistan, said he considers Chesty a "kindred soul."

"He's a fine Marine dog," the general said. "Loyal, hardworking and full of fun—while looking mean as all get-out."

Col. Montanus strenuously denies that the confrontation with Bravo helped Chesty's promotion. A well-trained Marine, he said, should be able to recognize a superior.

"I would say Chesty needs some threat-identification classes," he said. "I understand 'No better friend, no worse enemy.' But generally we are talking about our enemies, not our superior officers."

Col. Montanus calls the clash with Bravo a minor infraction. Chesty, the colonel says, excels at his main responsibility: accepting hugs from children with enthusiasm and without biting.

As for Bravo's master, there seem to be no hard feelings. "Chesty may bark a lot," Mr. Panetta said. "But he understands the chain of command."

In an interview on a hot evening, Chesty was friendly and panted constantly. Although he didn't answer questions about Bravo, he did jump on a reporter's leg.

Update

New Mascot
Takes Over

JULIAN E. BARNES

With his predecessor barking in either approval or protest, the Marine Corps' new mascot, Chesty XIV, was made a full Marine on April 8, 2013.

Top Marine officers urged the new mascot to carry on in the tradition of Sgt. Chesty XIII, while their wives are making sure the puppy is better behaved.

Bonnie Amos, the wife of Marine Commandant Gen. James Amos, has vowed the new mascot must be well-socialized and has been supervising his upbringing.

PFC Chesty XIV has been given good marks for his role as mascot sidekick this summer. In June, the two dogs paraded down the Center Walk of the Marine Barracks Washington for Army Gen. Martin Dempsey, the chairman of the Joint Chiefs of Staff.

"He still has a way to go, but he's been carrying out his duties to a high standard so far, and we expect his progress to continue on the right course," said Capt. John Norton, a spokesman for the Barracks.

On Ancient Pins
and Needles

ABIGAIL PESTA

Fonseca Bust

By day, Janet Stephens is a hairdresser at a Baltimore salon, trimming bobs and wispy bangs. By night she dwells in a different world. At home in her basement, with a mannequin head, she meticulously re-creates the hairstyles of ancient Rome and Greece.

Ms. Stephens is a hairdo archaeologist.

Her amateur scholarship is sticking a pin in the long-held assumptions among historians about the complicated, gravity-defying styles of ancient times. Basically, she has set out to prove that the ancients probably weren't wearing wigs after all.

"This is my hairdresserly grudge match with historical representations of hairstyles," says Ms. Stephens, who works at Studio 921 Salon & Day Spa, which offers circa 21st-century haircuts.

Her coiffure queries began, she says, when she was killing time in the Walters Art Museum in Baltimore back in 2001. A bust of the Roman empress Julia Domna caught her eye. "I thought, holy cow, that is so cool," she says, referring to the empress's braided bun, chiseled in stone. She wondered how it had been built. "It was amazing, like a loaf of bread sitting on her head," says Ms. Stephens.

She tried to re-create the 'do on a mannequin. "I couldn't get it to hold together," she says. Turning to the history books for clues, she learned that scholars widely believed the elaborately teased, towering and braided styles of the day were wigs.

She didn't buy that. Through trial and error she found that she could achieve the hairstyle by sewing the braids and bits together, using a needle. She dug deeper into art and fashion history books, looking for references to stitching.

In 2005, she had a breakthrough. Studying translations of Roman literature, Ms. Stephens says, she realized the Latin term "acus" was probably being misunderstood in the context of hairdressing. "Acus" has several meanings including a "single-prong hairpin" or "needle and thread," she says. Translators generally went with "hairpin."

The single-prong pins couldn't have held the intricate styles in place. But a needle and thread could. It backed up her hair hypothesis.

In 2007, she sent her findings to the *Journal of Roman Archaeology.* "It's amazing how much chutzpah you have when you have no idea what you're doing," she says. "I don't write scholarly material. I'm a hairdresser."

John Humphrey, the journal's editor, was intrigued. "I could tell even from the first version that it was a very serious piece of experimental archaeology which no scholar who was not a hairdresser—in other words, no scholar— would have been able to write," he says.

He showed it to an expert, who found the needle-and-thread theory "entirely original," says Mr. Humphrey, whose own scholarly work has examined arenas for Roman chariot racing.

Ms. Stephens' article was edited and published in 2008, under the headline "Ancient Roman Hairdressing: On (Hair)Pins and Needles." The only other article by a non-archaeologist that Mr. Humphrey can recall publishing in the journal's 25-year history was written by a soldier who had discovered an unknown Roman fort in Iraq.

Ms. Stephens dates her fascination with hair to her childhood in Kennewick, Wash., where she entertained herself as a five-year-old by cutting the neon tufts on her Troll dolls. When she chopped off all the Troll fluff and realized it wouldn't grow back, she says, she got into styling, creating Troll costumes including an Egyptian suit of armor made of tin foil. "Whatever you're most passionate about when you're five is what you should do for the rest of your life," says Ms. Stephens, 54 years old.

In recent years, Ms. Stephens has reconstructed the styles of ancient royals including Faustina the Younger and Empress Plotina—sometimes on live models. Last year she gave a presentation at an Archaeological Institute of America conference in Philadelphia in which she lined up several mannequin heads.

"It was like a bad science-fair project," she says. "I had

no idea what I was doing." Also speaking that day: a researcher with new insight into spearheads from the Iron Age in South Italy.

There is one hairstyle that Ms. Stephens says she hasn't been able to find a real, live model to submit to. The style, seen on an ancient Roman sculpture known as the Fonseca Bust, boasts a tall, horseshoe-shaped pile of curls in the front that would involve cutting the model's hair. "It's like a mullet from hell," she says.

At the cavernous, Buddha-filled Baltimore salon where Ms. Stephens is employed, her fellow stylists find her archaeology work a bit mysterious. Nevertheless, they occasionally model for her Roman re-creations.

One of them is Rachael Lynne Pietra. Her long tresses provided an ideal medium for demonstrating a style worn by the Vestal Virgins—women who took a vow of chastity and guarded a sacred fire in ancient Rome.

"People have been interested in the construction of that hairstyle for centuries," says Ms. Stephens. Big problem: Vestals wore their hair covered, so there are almost no carvings or images of the complete hairdo.

Ms. Stephens solved the mystery by studying many portraits, each showing bits of braids poking out from the front and back of the head covering. Then she "started scribbling" on the images, she says, "color-coding everything—this braid looks like it belongs with this one; that braid belongs with that one."

In a YouTube video by Ms. Stephens, "Vestal Hairdressing," she intones: "The Roman grammarian Festus informs us that both brides and the Vestal Virgins wore an ancient hairstyle called the Seni Crines."

The resulting nest of braids was "awesome," says Ms. Pietra, the model in the video. Although it did feel "heavy." She promptly took it down.

Ms. Stephens is "crazy, crazy intelligent," Ms. Pietra notes.

Not everyone agrees with the hairdresser's theories. Last month, at an Archaeological Institute of America conference in Seattle, Ms. Stephens says, a woman doing a dissertation on Vestal Virgin hair took issue with her argument that the Vestal hairstyle was built out of seven separate braids—not six as long believed.

"I walked her through it," Ms. Stephens says. "There's a logic to hair."

Marden Nichols, curator of ancient art at the Walters Art Museum, says Ms. Stephens is able to "break new ground" specifically because of her work as a stylist.

"Like many classicists, I spend my days analyzing works of literature and art that relate to activities I have never performed: harvesting crops, building temples, sacrificing animals," she says. Ms. Stephens can "draw upon practical experiences."

Thus far, none of Ms. Stephens's clients have asked her to do one of the ancient 'dos on them. But after her work appeared online, she says, "I did have a man fly down from Boston to get an Augustus Caesar cut."

Bird Battle

MICHAEL M. PHILLIPS

Del Johnson

BAGRAM AIRFIELD, Afghanistan—Flying an F-15E Eagle fighter may be the sexiest job the military has to offer.

The least sexy may be bagging up the beaks, talons and feathers smeared on the jet's exterior when an Eagle hits a sparrow at 500 miles per hour.

Lt. Col. Del Johnson does both. His day job is firing up the afterburners and flying combat missions out of Bagram, the main U.S. air base in Afghanistan. But as flight safety officer, his duties also include making sure that every time war bird and regular bird collide, the latter is scraped off the former and shipped to scientists at the Smithsonian Institution.

"It's not as glamorous a job as you might imagine," says Col. Johnson, a 38-year-old Kansan with a Top Gun grin and a 9mm pistol strapped to his shoulder.

A bird, even a small one, can bring down a $38 million F-15E fighter if it flies into the air intake and breaks the engine's turbine blades. A goose can smash through the canopy and do grievous injury to the two-man crew. Col. Johnson, for his part, once hit a vulture while flying at

500 feet above North Carolina. "I just saw a black bird," recalls the colonel, who landed safely. At 550 miles per hour, he says, "things go by pretty fast."

Bagram is on the Salang Corridor, a major Asian migration route, and the runway here is visited by raptors called black kites, as well as resident pigeons, doves, mynahs and sparrows. Since he began his combat tour in September, Col. Johnson has recorded more than 20 bird collisions involving planes from the 455th Air Expeditionary Wing.

The base has tried to persuade the birds to go elsewhere. Contractors used to burn garbage in open pits, but that attracted mice, and mice attracted birds. Now they burn trash in a towerlike structure. Sometimes, Col. Johnson shoots fireworks from a double-barreled signal pistol. He's also shopping for a laser to scare away birds. After ruling out a $995 Avian Dissuader model, he has his eye on a $7,700 Desman laser with a sniper's scope and 1.5-mile-long beam. (Birds aren't harmed by the laser, its dealer says.)

But one of the most reliable ways to avoid birds is for the pilots to learn their wily ways. That's where the Smithsonian comes in. Museum researchers identify bird remains and feed a database that helps the crews determine the hours and seasons when bird conditions are riskiest. "We use this data to analyze what we're hitting, where we're hitting and when we're hitting, so we can avoid them," says Col. Johnson.

In late October, two birds slammed into an F-15 at Bagram. One splattered just in front of the canopy and another hit the mount for the targeting pod, a $1 million piece of gear that allows pilots to see clear images of people and buildings tens of thousands of feet below, even in the dead of night.

The plane wasn't damaged. "There were no injuries," says Col. Johnson. "Well, there are two dead birds."

With a blue rag normally used to clean canopy windows, a ground crewman wiped tiny bits of bird off the plane and turned it over to Col. Johnson. He donned blue latex gloves and, as a precaution, poured alcohol over the sample to kill any avian flu virus. He double-bagged the remains, marked the specimen with the place, time and date of impact and packed it in a padded envelope with a series of documents, including proof of origin and a U.S. Department of Agriculture form allowing him to ship bird parts out of Afghanistan.

Birds downed by U.S. Air Force planes everywhere in the world end up in the morning mail of Carla Dove. Ms. Dove—yes, it's her real name and, yes, she gets the joke—is the program manager of the Feather Identification Lab at the National Museum of Natural History in Washington. A 45-year-old with feathered blond hair and a soft accent from her native Fulks Run, Va., Ms. Dove calls the morning delivery "snarge," a term of art that combines snot and garbage.

Smithsonian researchers have identified head-dress feathers for museum anthropologists and the contents of rattlesnake stomachs for naturalists. But most of their work is identifying birds killed by military planes. The lab team even ordered up its own souvenir coins, adopting a military tradition. "Got cherpies?" says one coin. "We'll tweet it."

Ms. Dove and her staff have three methods of identifying dead birds, which they do about 4,000 times a year. Marcy Heacker, a 44-year-old research assistant from Dayton, Ohio, specializes in matching whole feathers with those found on more than 620,000 bird specimens in the museum's back rooms. Red-tailed hawks, scarlet tanagers, blackpoll warblers and more are lined up in drawers stacked floor to ceiling, their bodies lifelike except for the white cotton where their eyes once were.

Last month, Ms. Heacker plucked a sack of feathers and a claw out of the morning mail, the remnants of a collision between a bird and a KC-135R, an airborne refueler, out of Altus Air Force Base in Oklahoma. The fluffy, peachy-beige breast feather immediately suggested a mourning dove. She climbed a ladder and pulled a stuffed one from a high drawer, holding it next to a white-tipped tail feather that looked as if it might have passed through a jet engine.

"Remember, this is a little chewed up," she said. "But it looks like a pretty good match."

When feather remains are too severely damaged to make a naked-eye identification, Ms. Dove steps in. In wooden filing drawers in her office, amid pictures of birds and jets, she keeps 2,400 microscope slides of fluffy feather barbs. Up close, she can see nodes that distinguish, say, a wren from a Muscovy duck. "Not many people do this," says Ms. Dove, who has worked at the lab for 19 years. "Nobody wants to go through the snarge."

Last year, a grateful pilot took Ms. Dove on a ride in an F-15. She proudly reports that, despite the flier's best efforts, she got through the flight without vomiting. She was alarmed, however, when someone told her afterward that a big red-tailed hawk had been perched on a nearby building as the plane took off. "Lucky I didn't see it or I would have told him to stop," she says.

In the case of Col. Johnson's two-bird specimen, however, there wasn't enough feather to do microscopic comparison. So the blue, blood-stained rag ended up with Nancy Rotzel, a 28-year-old molecular specialist from Appleton, Wis. Using an expensive machine provided by the Federal Aviation Administration, Ms. Rotzel extracted DNA from the sample and matched it to records from the Barcode of Life Data Systems, a collection of DNA from 35,105 plant and animal species.

The snarge revealed a 99.5% match with a skylark, and a 98.5% match with a great egret.

The Smithsonian team entered its findings into a global bird-avoidance database, which calculates the odds of a plane hitting a given species of bird at a given moment. Back at Bagram, the data help Col. Johnson set takeoff and landing schedules, at least within the constraints imposed by war.

"You have to go to the fight when the fight exists," he says. "So there's only so much you can do."

Question Mark Over the Apostrophes Future

BARRY NEWMAN

THURMAN, N.Y.—The Domestic Names Committee of the U.S. Board on Geographic Names doesn't like apostrophes. Visitors to Harpers Ferry or Pikes Peak might not realize it, but anyone aspiring to name a ridge or a swamp after a local hero will soon find out.

In this Adirondack town, pop. 1,219, a move is on to put a mountain on the map in honor of James Cameron, who settled here in 1773. There is some dispute as to which mountain, and whether to call it Jimmy's Peak, Jimmie's Peak or James' Peak. But there is no opposition to the apostrophe—except from the government.

"Without it, Jimmys looks plural, not possessive," Evelyn Wood, Thurman's town supervisor, said one morning upstairs in the Town Hall. She is 35 years old and has a college degree in English. The Domestic Names Committee, citing her "Jimmy's Peak" proposal in a letter, added "[sic]" after each "Jimmy's."

Said Ms. Wood, "They're their '[sics]' not ours."

For punctuation sticklers, this official apostrophe aversion is a sad comment on a useful mark in serious trouble.

Apostrophes aren't welcome on the Web (McDonald's is mcdonalds.com). Banks and druggists ignore them (Barclays, Walgreens). And they sow signage chaos (Employee's Only; Happy Bosses Day; Blue's Band).

"This adds to illiteracy," says Persis Granger, founder of the Adirondack Mountain Writers' Retreat, which meets here in Thurman every July.

Among other English speakers, place-name apostrophes are all over the map: Bushmans Kloof in South Africa and Campbell's Bay in Canada. In England, Mid Devon's council voted this year to expunge apostrophes from street signs. It backed down after an outcry from the Apostrophe Protection Society.

The U.S., in fact, is the only country with an apostrophe-eradication policy. The program took off when President Benjamin Harrison set up the Board on Geographic Names in 1890. By one board estimate, it has scrubbed 250,000 apostrophes from federal maps. The states mostly—but not always—bow to its wishes.

An apostrophe, the argument goes, implies private ownership of a public place. When names appear on maps, "they change from words having specific dictionary meaning to fixed labels used to refer to geographic entities," the names committee explains in its statement of "Principles, Policies and Procedures."

Irish names (O'Fallon, Ill.) and French ones (Coeur d'Alene, Idaho) aren't possessives and get by. While administrative names can endure (Prince George's County,

Md.), the committee has granted only five possessive apostrophes in 113 years: Martha's Vineyard, Mass.; Ike's Point, N.J.; John E's Pond, R.I.; Carlos Elmer's Joshua View, Ariz.; and—in 2002—Clark's Mountain, Ore.

What the names committee didn't do in banning the apostrophe was to ban the "s" that follows it. So you can't tell if Pikes Peak was named for a Pike or a Pikes. Here in New York, the same applies to Howes Cave, Coeymans Hollow, Watkins Glen and Yonkers.

The no-apostrophe rule has been reaffirmed five times, yet punctuationists fight on. At a 2009 meeting with place namers from the states, the names committee was flayed for its "isolationist stance" toward "the perpetually punished apostrophe."

"The apostrophe has a function," says Thomas Gasque, an English professor who spent years on South Dakota's Geographic Names Authority. "It can imply things other than possession," he says. "We talk about a winter's day. The day doesn't belong to winter."

As Prof. Gasque sees it, map makers should prize locally used apostrophes as mainstays of history. "Place names are the autobiography of a nation," he says.

Tell that to Theodore Roosevelt. In 1906, he ordered the standardization of geographic names for federal use. For the sake of consistency, there was no going back. Jennifer Runyon, one of the name committee's three staffers, says: "We don't debate the apostrophe."

The committee gets no flak from A.J. Sartin, who wants

a stretch of Florida coastline named "Veterans Island." "It's the way to do it on the Web," he says. Nor did Marc Maria object when denied an apostrophe for "Patriot's Peak," a nubble he owns in Maine. "It was a reference to a lot of people," Mr. Maria says, adding, "I've lost track of grammar, I guess."

In Thurman, the apostrophe is showing more gumption. People here long identified a peak with the old settler, James Cameron, and spelled its name with an apostrophe. Yet it never got onto a map.

In 2010, Susan Jennings, 62, a schoolteacher and Cameron descendant, applied to have a mountain she can see from her porch named "Jimmy's Peak." The names committee nixed the apostrophe. Ms. Jennings didn't argue.

"You don't pronounce apostrophes," she said, looking across the Hudson River at the mountain one day. "So it makes perfect sense."

But when the name hit the news, Lillie Cameron was shocked. She is 82 years old and a Cameron clan member. She says the government not only forgot the apostrophe— it named the wrong mountain.

Upstairs in the Town Hall with Ms. Wood, Thurman's supervisor, Ms. Cameron opened a handwritten book, dated 1906. The title page read: "Roster of the James' Peak Mountain Club." The next page was headed, "Jimmie's Peak Mountain Club Resolutions." A map indicated that the peak referred to is one mountain to the south.

In March, after Ms. Cameron's formal protest, the

names committee voted to consider deleting "Jimmys Peak" from its latest digital maps. As a punctuation-neutral substitute, it has in mind a name nobody here seems to recognize: Willard Mountain.

The peak that the mountain club called Jimmie's (or James') somehow has another official name: Bald Mountain. Rest assured that the Domestic Names Committee has no intention of changing it now.

"I'd still like it called Jimmy's," said Ms. Cameron, agreeing with Ms. Wood on spelling it that way. "I'd like it on the map."

"But as long as it's not on the map," Ms. Wood told her, "here in Thurman we can still call it Jimmy's Peak—with the apostrophe."

STUFF

Grab Your "Murse"

CHRISTINA PASSARIELLO AND RAY A. SMITH

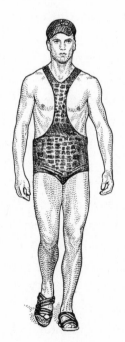

Emporio Armani mankini

The fashion industry has its knickers in a twist over "manties."

A contraction of "man" and "panties," the wordplay is meant to describe certain undergarments for males.

It's part of a special lexicon that has emerged, over the past decade, as a sort of shorthand for men's fashion. Men can also wear "mandals" (male sandals), "murses" (purses), "mantyhose" (pantyhose) and "mankinis" (swimsuit variants)—though not necessarily all at the same time.

At first, the neologisms were a kind of secret language among the fashion industry, etymologists say. Yet they're going mainstream. Now, editors of the prestigious Oxford English Dictionary are tracking them for possible inclusion.

The men's collection shows at New York Fashion Week, which kicks off Thursday, could give rise to more neologisms. Fashion editors often lack the words to describe wacky runway concoctions.

At Hermes' women's fashion collection in March, for example, "poots" was coined to identify a pair of leather pants that segue into boots.

But not everyone is thrilled about the emerging vocabulary. Some fashion types complain that it's emasculating.

"Manties is pretty high on the repellent meter," says Glenn O'Brien, author of "How To Be A Man" and a style advice columnist at *GQ* magazine.

Ross McCammon, an editor at *Esquire* who oversees the men's magazine's Vocabulary column, says, "We're interested in pushing the language forward and don't think there's a new way to use 'man' or 'bro.'" Such prefixes help to promote a "cartoonish idea of men," he says.

The invention of new words to describe men's fashion is a symptom of the recent boom in the men's fashion industry. The sector is proving particularly resilient to economic turbulence: During the first half of this year, sales of men's apparel in the U.S. rose 4.6% while women's fell 0.8%, according to market researcher NPD Group.

Mewelry (that's jewelry for men, not for cats) is also on the rise. Pinky rings have met their match in wristbands. They come in leather from Tod's—a favorite of bankers—and woven versions in string and cotton from Burkman Bros.

Then there are mandals—open-toed shoes that are more formal and structured than flip-flops. President Barack Obama was spotted in a black pair last summer. Yet the presidential footgear was immediately panned by style watchers. "They're ugly," declared fashion/celebrity blog Jezebel. Other online critics were squeamish over seeing Mr. Obama's toes.

Most designers wouldn't dream of using the new descriptors. "If it makes you happy to wear sandals, go for it—but I wouldn't call them mandals," says Umit Benan, the winner of the inaugural "Who Is On Next?" Italian competition for up-and-coming men's wear designers.

Linguists see the new vocabulary as an emancipation of sorts of men's fashion. And they're taking it seriously.

In the same way that the "e-" prefix was added to words such as store and bank to designate their online existence, "man" is used to describe the masculine version of inherently feminine objects, says Erin McKean, the founder of Wordnik.com, a website for word enthusiasts.

The rise of men's fashion, and its corresponding lexicon, goes back to the birth of the term "metrosexual" in the 1990s. Used to describe a man who is concerned with his appearance, it ushered in a generation of pop culture stars like Justin Timberlake, Joe Jonas and Kanye West who are praised, not ridiculed, for their style choices.

"Suddenly, there's this way of talking about [men's appearance] which could occasionally be complimentary," says Cynthia Miller, a lecturer on popular culture at Emerson College in Boston. "It became part of the popular consciousness."

That didn't make men's garment choices immune to humor, she notes. In a 1995 "Seinfeld" episode, the character Kramer invents a contraption called a "bro" or "manssiere" as a potential remedy for heavy-chested males. More recently, manties were spoofed on "Saturday Night Live."

A few expressions deal with the less glamorous side of fashion. Some male models are said to suffer from "manorexia." Several words describe grooming more than fashion, such as "guyliner" (eyeliner for guys) and "manscaping" (the removal of hair from men's limbs and loins).

In the past decade, manbag has become particularly common—both as a product and as a word. Department store chain Macy's has carved out space for manbags in some of its biggest stores, doubling its selection over the past year. Macy's men's fashion director Durand Guion says pockets just don't suffice for carrying an iPod, iPad and cellphone.

But he would never call the things manbags—or murses. "I don't like terms that mock this trend," Mr. Guion says. "I like terms that define the specific bag: messenger, gym, tote, carryall, backpack, portfolio, duffel."

The folks over at Oxford English Dictionary take a different view. They gave "manbag" a stamp of approval five years ago—the only new men's fashion term to receive the distinction. Fiona McPherson, the dictionary's senior editor for new words, said manbag had met the test of time. She traced the word's first use back to 1968.

Ms. McPherson said the OED requires "evidence of a word's usage over a 10-year period, before considering it for inclusion" in its editions. That criteria so far disqualifies a synonym for "manbag," "murse," as well as "mankini," "mandals" and "manties." None of them go back further than a decade, she said.

To the consternation of the fashion industry, the new terms are redefining fashion faux pas. The British beach town of Newquay has witnessed a rise in mankini violations, according to chief of Newquay Police Ian Drummond-Smith. This summer, for example, a man was reprimanded on an English beach for wearing a thong-like suit with a halter strap similar to the one made famous by Borat, the fictional Kazak journalist.

Mr. Drummond-Smith said the slinky one-piece breached Britain's Section 5 of Public Order Act 1986, "which prohibits the display of items likely to cause harassment, alarm & distress."

The Infidelity Phone

DAISUKE WAKABAYASHI

Fujitsu F-03 phone

TOKYO—Over the past few years, as many people rushed to trade in their old phones for smartphones, Japan's philanderers have remained faithful to one particular brand: Fujitsu Ltd.'s older "F-Series" phones, which feature some attractive stealth privacy features.

The aging flip-phone—nicknamed the "uwaki keitai" or "infidelity phone"—owes its enduring popularity to customers who don't believe newer smartphones are as discreet at hiding their illicit romances.

A Japanese blogger who goes by the name Bakanabe and writes anonymously about picking up women said he looked into buying a new device but found the privacy settings fell short of his current phone. Instead, he opted to refurbish his battered, three-year-old Fujitsu flip-phone with a new casing and a new battery.

"Women may want to check my phone for strange emails or calls when I'm not around. With Fujitsu's 'privacy mode,' they can't see that information at all," he said in an email. "The key is to give off the impression that you're not locking your phone at all."

Fujitsu's "privacy mode" is a layer of nearly invisible security that hides missed calls, emails and text messages from contacts designated as private. If one of those acquaintances gets in touch, the only signal of that communication is a subtle change in the color or shape of how the battery sign or antenna bars are displayed. If ignored, the call doesn't appear in the phone log.

The changes are so subtle that it would be impossible to spot for an untrained eye. When the privacy mode is turned off through a secret combination of keys, the concealed calls and messages appear, and voice mail becomes accessible.

This comes in handy to another blogger who calls himself "Poza." He claims to have various romances on dating sites while juggling three girlfriends. He said he was introduced to the Fujitsu phone nearly five years ago and uses the privacy features to keep from getting caught. He says he recently bought an iPhone, but giving up his Fujitsu phone to carry just a smartphone is "unthinkable."

"In terms of keeping my cheating hidden, this does more than enough," he wrote in an email. Poza, who says he works for a design company in western Japan, declined to provide his real name.

The older Japanese phones also run on software created for the domestic market. For years, this gave the manufacturers significant control over new features but limited their international reach. With smartphones running Google Inc.'s Android operating system—the main software option for today's handsets—the Japanese makers don't have as much control to develop new features.

Fujitsu started offering the privacy mode in 2002 as part of more stringent security requirements for all phones offered by NTT DoCoMo Inc., Japan's largest carrier. Takeshi Natsuno, a senior DoCoMo executive at the time, said he insisted on tougher security after hearing too many stories of couples splitting or workers landing in hot water because they left their phones out and unguarded.

"If Tiger Woods had this Japanese feature in his phone, he wouldn't have gotten in trouble," said Mr. Natsuno, now a professor at Keio University's Graduate School of Media and Governance.

The phones, though, aren't available outside Japan.

With emails, phone calls and text messages all coming into the phone, it is also where many affairs are carried out. Toshiyuki Makiguchi, who runs Uwaki Rescue SOS, a Tokyo-based consulting company to help people find out if their partners are cheating, said more than half of his 600 customers a year find some evidence of cheating on their partner's mobile phone.

Fujitsu promotes the strong security of its phones, but does so without acknowledging its subset of loyal cheater fans. Fujitsu spokesman Naoki Mishiro said tight security is critical these days with so much sensitive information on handsets. He declined to comment on the infidelity phone nickname.

These days, the devotion of infidelity phone users is being tested. Both Japanese carriers and Fujitsu are starting to phase out the older phones for an all-smartphone lineup. And a growing number of so-called cheater apps are looking to bring similar functions to smartphones.

As a result, Fujitsu has added some of the privacy features to its smartphone lineup. The company's new models conceal calls and emails from contacts marked private. Like its older cousin, it alerts the users with a subtle change in the battery or antenna mark. However, the privacy mode requires a separate mail and address book app designed by Fujitsu, rather than the default email program and address book provided by the carrier.

"It's totally useless," said blogger Bakanabe, who researched the Fujitsu smartphone before sticking with his existing phone. "I hold out hope that Fujitsu adds the real privacy mode with its next smartphone."

Fujitsu said it aims to roll out more convenient and secure features in the future.

The world appears to be catching up with the infidelity phone.

Delaware-based CATE, or Call and Text Eraser, has been offering a similar level of security since last year. It is an app for Android-based smartphones that intercepts and hides text messages and phone calls from people on a selected "blacklist." Those texts and calls, as well as the app itself, remain hidden until the user punches in a code.

"I believe most cheaters use text and get caught by the text," said Neal Desai, a 25-year-old entrepreneur from

Austin, Texas, who raised $70,000 for the $4.99 app on ABC's reality TV show "Shark Tank."

At $4.99 per download, CATE has been downloaded more than 10,000 times, and an iPhone version will be available soon, said Mr. Desai.

When told about Fujitsu's privacy features that have been available in Japan for several years, Mr. Desai was impressed: "That's more genius than my app."

MIHO INADA CONTRIBUTED TO THIS ARTICLE.

Banking on
Authors' Clutter

BARRY NEWMAN

HADLEY, Mass.—The Green Library at Stanford University houses William Saroyan's mustache clippings. Timothy Leary's Nintendo Power Glove has been acquired by the New York Public Library. At the Harry Ransom Center of the University of Texas at Austin, Norman Mailer's bar mitzvah speech is preserved in perpetuity.

Authors, take notice: Remember those crates of scratch pads and tax returns in the garage? The trunkful of hotel bills and childhood doodles in the garden shed? Don't junk any of it—not before you call up somebody in Ken Lopez's line of work.

Mr. Lopez, who has a book-jammed office in this small town, is a broker—one of a dozen in the country—who deals in the flotsam of authorship. He sells to rich research libraries, which sort it and shelve it so scholars can mine it for clues to creativity.

"If you had William Faulkner's laundry list, would you care?" Mr. Lopez said not long ago. "The answer is, 'Yes.' So if it's true for Faulkner," he added rhetorically, "it could be true for you."

Being dead helps but isn't required. Mailer sold his 1,062 boxes for $2.5 million in 2005 and died in 2007. In 2003, Bob Woodward and Carl Bernstein sold 83 Watergate boxes, also to the Ransom, for $5 million. After 20 years of marketing for the likes of William S. Burroughs (dead) and Peter Matthiessen (alive), Mr. Lopez puts prices for interesting paper piles at $30,000 to $300,000.

His emphasis is on the paper. Digitization has made correspondence more searchable but less revealing. Still, Wendy Cope, a poet of light verse, recently sold the British Library 40,000 emails for $50,000. "A lot of them are extremely boring," she told the BBC. One of her poems explains why. "Don't answer emails," it goes, "when you're drunk."

Typescripts that used to be cut, pasted and blue-penciled are spotlessly digital now. Word processing has obscured the process of writing. "The archaeology of it, seeing paths not taken," Mr. Lopez said early one Monday. "At this point, that'll all be lost."

Long-haired and 60 years old, he had just driven a Penske rental truck from Arizona with the trove of a Native American writer, N. Scott Momaday. His office this day was crowded with the uncensored (and as yet unsold) dispatches of George Weller, a reporter who sneaked into Nagasaki after the atomic bomb dropped. In tight quarters, Mr. Lopez repacked Mr. Momaday and got him on the road again—for New Haven.

Yale University's Beinecke Library would be the new

home of the Momaday archive—100 boxes of manuscripts and shopping lists. "I wish I'd kept it all in longhand," says Mr. Momaday, who is 78 and lives in Florida now. "It would have been much more valuable." Yale won't name its price. Mr. Momaday will: $500,000. Mr. Lopez gets 15%.

Once, writers like Mr. Momaday gave their stuff away. But in 1969, Congress ended tax deductions for creators of their own gifts. Richard Nixon signed the law and, in donating his papers, ran afoul of it himself when his advisers tried to claim a deduction after the law took effect. Dozens of libraries with big budgets have since been bidding up the stashes in authorial attics. Hundreds, less endowed, are left with shelf space reserved for literary altruists.

"Authors would love for us to have their archives, but they want to sell," says Chantel Dunham, who raises money for the University of Georgia's libraries in Athens, Ga. "People ask for hundreds of thousands. We're a state institution. We can't pay anything like that."

Emory University, 65 miles away in Atlanta, can. In 2006, for an undisclosed amount, Salman Rushdie sold it 200 "falling apart, crappy cardboard boxes," as he said at the collection's opening in 2010. After Emory's archivists put his "mess" in order, Mr. Rushdie capitalized on their tidiness to research his own 2012 memoir.

Some authors, like Philip Roth, say they want their scribbles burned after they die, so the public won't root through them. (Kafka tried that; it didn't work.) Some toss their trash, like ordinary folk do. A few devote deep thoughts to the fate of their Post-it Notes.

"What if I'm one of those people that people study?" says Ronlyn Domingue. "What am I going to leave behind for them?"

Ms. Domingue, who is 43 and lives in Baton Rouge, has one published novel with two on the way. She writes in longhand, types it up, makes changes by hand and dumps it all into a box in her closet marked "Archive." She has willed the box to Louisiana State University, her alma mater. "I never thought of asking for money for it," she says.

Ms. Domingue hasn't met Mr. Lopez.

"A lot of writers don't know about this market," he was saying as he backed the Penske truck into a dock at a Yale warehouse and delivered Mr. Momaday's crates into the hands of their buyers.

Four archivists wheeled them into a room of wood-topped tables. Mike Rush lifted the lid on Mr. Momaday's LP records. "The first few minutes get your heart racing," he said, flipping through them.

On the floor and surrounding shelves, the accumulations of others were in early stages of screening. A box from a photographer, Lee Friedlander, had recently yielded a salt shaker that contained a grayish powder. It turned out to be the ashes of Robert Heinecken, an artist who died in 2006, mailed on his behalf as a posthumous gift.

"That was fun," said Mr. Rush, reaching into playwright John Guare's cache. He extracted an envelope from which slid five watches and three wallets, one containing a note for 200 Greek drachmas. Mr. Rush said, "We get uncashed checks. We send them back, if recent."

The Beinecke doesn't make its own checkbook public, but it buys enough stuff each year to fill 1,000 feet of shelving; 7,000 feet of it has yet to be cataloged. So Mr. Momaday's boxes would have to wait their turn.

Mr. Rush, however, was taking one step right away: Bagging them up to be left for three days, at 30 degrees below zero, in Yale's industrial blast freezer. It's one thing to buy the contents of a living writer's cellar, but the Beinecke Library had to be sure that nothing else Mr. Lopez sold it was still alive.

About the Editor

Barry Newman, a New Yorker, joined *The Wall Street Journal* in 1970. In 43 years as a staff reporter, he wrote more than 400 feature stories for the front page from more than 65 countries. He is a winner of the Overseas Press Club's award for explanatory journalism and the National Press Club's award for humor writing. His stories have been collected in several books, including *East of the Equator, The Literary Journalists* and *Floating Off the Page.* He is at work on a new collection of stories from *The Journal,* combined with essays on how he reported and wrote them, to be published by CUNY Journalism Press.